Daniel Miranda Huerta

713 278 7322

1000 FACTS ON
PREHISTORIC LIFE

Barnes & Noble Publishing, Inc.
122 Fifth Avenue
New York, NY 10011

ISBN 0-7607-6844-7

Printed and bound in China

05 06 07 08 09 MCH 10 9 8 7 6 5 4 3 2 1

Library of Congress Cataloging-in-Publication Data available upon request.

Editorial Director: Belinda Gallagher Assistant Editor: Hannah Todd
Designer: Tom Slemmings Production: Estela Boulton
Americanization: Jenni Rainford

Scanning and Reprographics: Anthony Cambray,
Mike Coupe, Ian Paulyn

1000 FACTS ON
PREHISTORIC LIFE

Andrew Campbell
Consultant: Steve Parker

BARNES & NOBLE BOOKS
NEW YORK

Contents

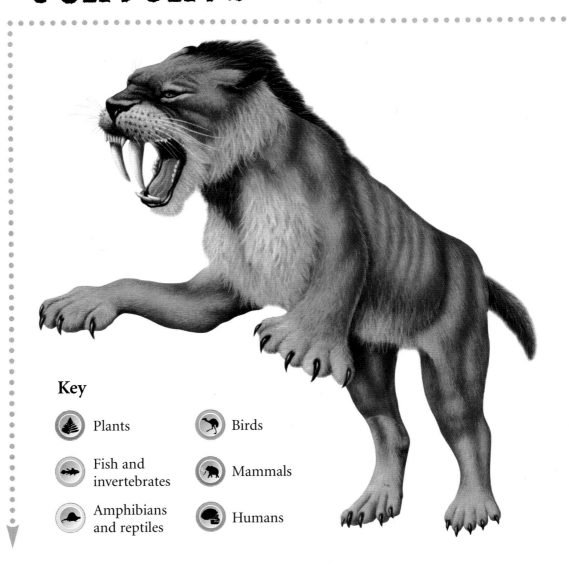

Key

Contents

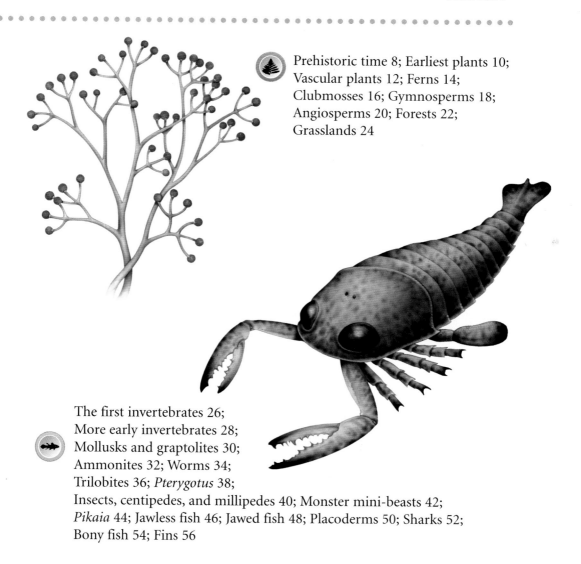

Contents

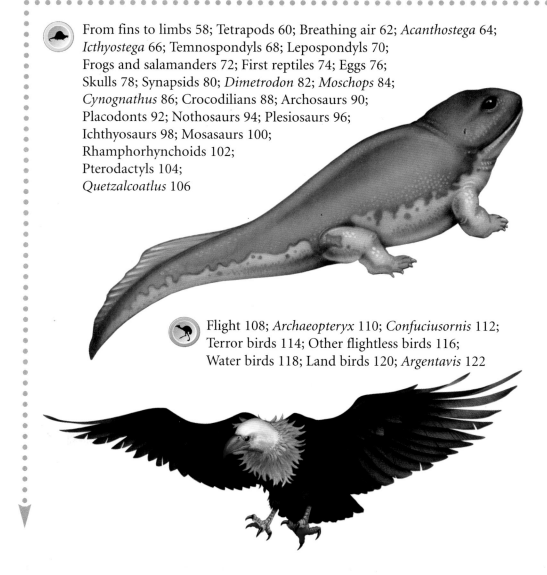

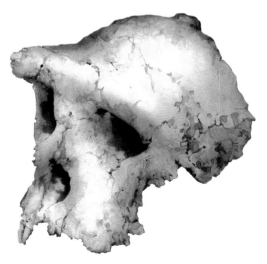

Prehistoric time

- **Time since the Earth formed** is divided into large units called eras, which are in turn divided into periods. Some periods split further into epochs. These units of time relate to the formation of rock layers.

- **The Precambrian Era** ran from 4,600–542 million years ago (mya). It saw the beginning of life in the seas. In the Cambrian Period (542–490 mya) the seas were dominated by the first vertebrates.

- **During the Ordovician Period** (490–435 mya) plants spread to land. In the Silurian Period (435–410 mya) the first jawed fish appeared, together with the first upright-standing land plants.

- **The Devonian Period** (410–355 mya) witnessed the development of bony fish in the seas, and trees and insects on land.

- **The Carboniferous Period** (355–298 mya) was the time of the great tropical forests and the first land animals with backbones.

- **During the Permian Period** (298–250 mya) reptiles became the major land creatures.

- **The Triassic Period** (250–208 mya) saw the rise of the dinosaurs and the first small mammals. In the Jurassic Period (208–144 mya) reptiles dominated the land, sea, and sky.

- **The Cretaceous Period** (144–65 mya) saw the proliferation of flowering plants, but its end also saw the extinction of the dinosaurs.

- **The Tertiary Period** (65–1.6 mya) saw the successful development of mammals and grassland habitats, and cooling temperatures.
- **The Quaternary Period** (1.6 mya–present) has witnessed the most recent series of ice ages and the rise of modern humans.

▼ *Even though many kinds of animals and plants died out 65 mya, other groups lived on. Insects, worms, fish, birds and mammals all survived the mass extinction – and these groups are still alive today.*

Earliest plants

- **The very first** living things on Earth were single-celled bacteria and cyanobacteria, also known as blue-green algae.

- **Blue-green algae** emerged around 3,500 mya.

▲ *Lichens such as these are made up of an alga and fungus. Early lichens—like modern-day ones—grew on rocks and, over time, eroded part of the rock and helped to form soil.*

- **Although it is not** a plant, blue-green algae contains chlorophyll and was the first living thing to photosynthesize (make energy from sunlight).

- **Photosynthesis** also produces oxygen. Over millions of years, the blue-green algae produced enough oxygen to enable more complex life forms to develop.

- **True algae**, which are usually regarded as plants, developed around 1,000 mya.

- **By about** 550 mya, multi-celled plants had begun to appear, including simple seaweeds.

- **Algae and lichens** were the first plants to appear on land.

- **Bryophyte plants** (mosses and liverworts) emerged on land around 440 mya. Bryophytes are simple green seedless plants.

- **Bryophytes** cannot grow high above the ground because they do not have strengthened stems, unlike vascular plants, which emerged later.

...FASCINATING FACT...
Liverworts grew on mats of blue-green algae, which trapped nitrogen from the air. Liverworts used this nitrogen to grow tissues.

Vascular plants

- **Vascular plants have branching stems** with tubelike walls that carry water and nutrients.

- **They** are more suited to living on drier land than mosses and liverworts.

- **These stems** and walls also mean that the plants can stand tall. Vascular plants have spores (reproductive cells, like seeds)—the taller the plant, the more widely it can disperse its spores.

- **One of the first known** vascular plants was *Cooksonia*. It was about 2 in (5 cm) tall, with a forked stem.

- **Scientists** called paleontologists discovered fossil remains of *Cooksonia* in Wales. Paleontologists study fossils of prehistoric plants and animals to see how they lived and evolved.

- **One site** where lots of vascular plant fossils have been found is Rhynie in Scotland.

- **The plants** at Rhynie would have grown on the sandy edges of pools in the Early Devonian Period (about 400 mya).

- **One plant fossil** found at Rhynie is *Aglaophyton*, which stood around 18 in (45 cm) high.

- *Aglaophyton* had underground roots and tissues that supported the plant stem. It also had water-carrying tubes and stomata (tiny openings) that allowed air and water to pass through.

- **Land-living plants** were essential for providing conditions for animals to make the transition from the seas to land. They created soil, food, and ground cover for shelter.

▶ *The* Cooksonia *plant had forked stems ending in spore-filled caps. The earliest examples of* Cooksonia *have been found in Ireland, dating to around 430 mya.*

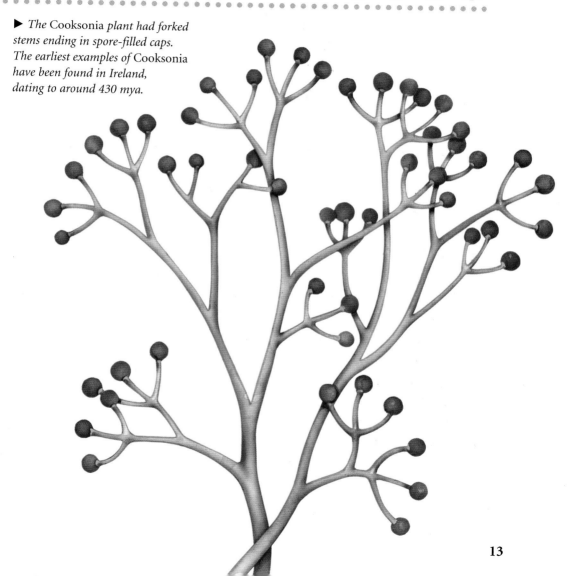

Ferns

- **Ferns** are flowerless, spore-producing plants, with roots, stems, and, leaves called fronds.
- **They developed** from the earliest vascular plants, such as *Cooksonia*.
- **Ferns** first appeared in the Devonian Period (410–355 mya).
- *Cladoxylon* was an early, primitive fern. It had a main stem, forked branches and leaves, and fan-shaped structures that contained spores.
- **During the Carboniferous Period** (355–298 mya), ferns became some of the most abundant plants on Earth.
- **Prehistoric ferns** would have looked similar to modern ones, but they could grow much larger. Large ferns are called tree ferns.
- **Sometimes paleontologists** find many fossilized fern spores in a single layer of rock. These "fern spikes" show that there were a lot of ferns around at a particular time.
- **There is a major fern spike** from rock layers that are around 65 million years old, when many other plants had died out, along with dinosaurs and other animals. This fern spike shows that ferns were not affected by the extinctions.
- **Ferns** are great survivors—after volcanic eruptions, they are the first plants to grow again in a landscape.

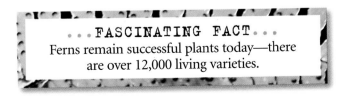

...FASCINATING FACT...
Ferns remain successful plants today—there
are over 12,000 living varieties.

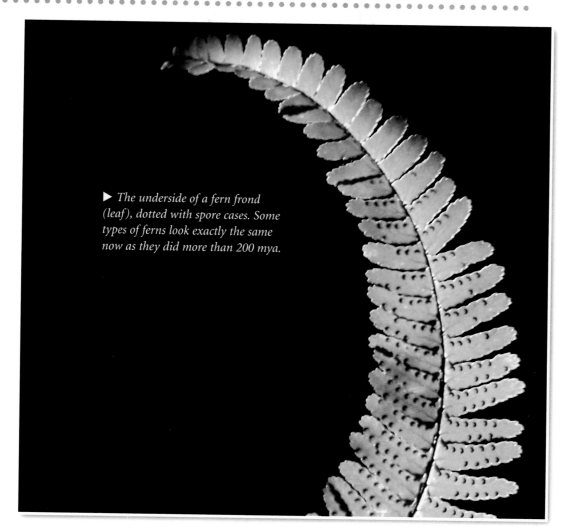

▶ The underside of a fern frond
(leaf), dotted with spore cases. Some
types of ferns look exactly the same
now as they did more than 200 mya.

Clubmosses

- **Clubmosses** are covered with tiny spiral-patterned leaves. Near the top of the stem are club-shaped structures that produce spores.

- **Clubmosses** started to grow on moist ground in the Devonian Period (410–355 mya).

- **Early clubmosses** included *Protolepidodendrum, Baragwanathia,* and *Sawdonia.*

- **Another early clubmoss** was *Asteroxylon.* It had forked branches with tiny leaves called leaflets.

- **By the Late Devonian Period**, clubmosses evolved into much bigger forms and produced the first tree-sized plants, such as *Lepidodendron.*

- *Lepidodendron* **trees** could grow more than 98ft (30 m) high. The diameter of their trunks could be over 7 ft (2 m).

- *Lepidodendron* grew all over the world in the Carboniferous Period (355–298 mya).

- **It produced** large spores inside coneshaped containers.

- **Some clubmosses** survive to this day, including *Lycopodium.*

▶ *Fossilized* Lepidodendron *bark shows that the trunks of these giant clubmosses were covered in diamond-shaped patterns.* Lepidodendron *leaves could be up to 3 ft (1 m) long, and its roots stretched out for up to 39 ft (12 m).*

....FASCINATING FACT....
Along with tree-ferns, clubmosses were the first treesized plants. They were supported by the first well-developed underground roots.

Gymnosperms

- **Gymnosperms** are plants that produce exposed seeds on the surface of structures such as cones. The word gymnosperm comes from two Greek words: *gymnos*, meaning, "naked", and *sperma*, meaning "seed."

- **They first appeared** about 370 mya. Like ferns, they probably developed from early plants such as *Cooksonia*.

- **Gymnosperms** grew well in the damp, tropical forests of the Carboniferous Period (355–298 mya).

- **Varieties** of gymnosperm include conifers, cycads, and seed ferns.

- **Cycads** are palmlike plants with feathery tops. They were much more common in prehistoric times than today.

- **One type** of cycad is the maidenhair tree, *Gingko biloba*. It still grows in towns and cities, but is now very rare in the wild.

- **One extinct gymnosperm** is *Glossopteris*, which some palaeontologists believe is the ancestor of later flowering plants.

- **Together with** ferns and horsetails (a type of herb), gymnosperms dominated landscapes during the Mesozoic Era (250–65 mya).

▶ *This* Araucaria, *or monkey puzzle tree, is a type of conifer that dates back to the Jurassic Period (208–144 mya).*

- **In the Jurassic Period** (208–144 mya), plant-eating dinosaurs ate their way through huge areas of coniferous forest.

- **In response**, conifers developed tough leaves, sharp needles, and poisons.

▲ *These modern pine cones each surround many individual seeds. When the seeds are ripe, the cones open so that the seeds can fall out. Early gymnosperms had less sophisticated seed containers, which consisted of forked branches that loosely held the seeds in place.*

Angiosperms

- **Angiosperms** are flowering plants. They produce seeds within an ovary, which is contained within a flower. The word comes from the Greek terms *angeion*, meaning "vessel," and *sperma*, meaning "seed."

- **Angiosperms** first appeared about 140 mya.

- **The earliest evidence** of flowering plants comes from the fossil remains of leaves and pollen grains.

- **Plant experts** used to think that magnolias were one of the first angiosperms, but now they think that an extinct plant called *Archaefructus* was older. It lived about 145 mya.

- **Fossil remains** of *Archaefructus* were discovered in northeast China in the mid to late 1990s.

- **By 100 mya,** angiosperms had developed into many dozens of families of flowering plants, most of which still survive today.

- **By 60 mya,** angiosperms had taken over from gymnosperms as the dominant plants on Earth.

- **The start of the Tertiary Period** (around 65 mya) saw a rise in temperatures that produced the right conditions for tropical rain forests.

- **It was in the rain forests** that angiosperms evolved into many, many different types of plants.

- **Angiosperms** became so successful because they could grow very quickly, they had very extensive root systems to anchor them and take up water and nutrients, and they could grow in a greater range of environments than other plants, such as gymnosperms.

▶ *An* Archaefructus *plant, which some scientists think is the earliest-known example of an angiosperm. The* Archaefructus *fossil, which may be around 145 million years old, has a number of angiosperm features including enclosed seeds and flowers.*

21

Forests

- **The Carboniferous Period** (355–298 mya) was the time of the greatest forests on Earth.

- **The damp climate** of this period suited forests, as did the huge number of swamps in which many trees grew.

- **Carboniferous forests** contained huge clubmosses, growing up to 164 ft (50 m) tall, as well as tree ferns and primitive conifers, such as *Archaeopteris*.

- **The huge numbers** of enormous trees in this period produced the highest levels of oxygen there has ever been on Earth.

- **Dead forest trees** fell and formed mats of rotting wood, which over time turned into peat.

- **Layers of sandstone** or other rock formed over the peat. The pressure of these new layers eventually caused the peat to dry and harden into coal.

- **Coal deposits** are rich sources of fossilized animals.

- **In later periods,** following the Carboniferous Period, plant-eating dinosaurs ate their way through huge areas of forest.

- **Forests** were home to many prehistoric animals, including the first small mammals, such as *Megazostrodon* and *Morganucodon*, which could hide from predators among the trees.

- **By the Tertiary Period** (65–1.6 mya), forests contained many more deciduous (leaf-shedding) trees, such as magnolias, than evergreens, such as conifers.

▼ *Two plant-eating sauropod dinosaurs (Jobaria left, and Janenschia right) eating the branches at the tops of trees in a forest of the late Jurassic Period (159–144 mya). These forests had developed millions of years earlier, during the Carboniferous Period.*

23

Grasslands

- **In the Oligocene Epoch** (37–24 mya), the Earth's climate became cooler, causing the ice cap covering Antarctica to increase in size.

- **As a result**, tropical rain forests began to decline and grasslands became increasingly common.

- **Grasslands** are called many things in different parts of the world: plains, savannas, steppes, veldt, and prairies.

- **The change** from one ecosystem to another, such as forest to grassland, is called succession. It is a continual process and in central Australia, for example, prehistoric grasslands have been succeeded by desert.

- **Grasses** provided an abundant source of food.

- **Unlike many** other plants, grasses can be cropped without destroying the plant itself, so they provide animals with a constant supply of food.

▼ *Etosha National Park, Namibia, South Africa. Grasses did not appear on Earth until around 50 mya. Their ability to withstand drought, fire and grazing are part of the reason why they spread so successfully across the world.*

- **Grasses** are tougher than soft forest plants. This meant that plant eaters had to develop stronger teeth and better digestive systems.

- **The open nature** of grasslands meant that mammals had to become faster runners, too—to chase after prey or to escape predators.

- **About 11,000 years ago** temperatures began to rise and many grasslands dried out. Lush, mixed grasses gave way to much coarser grasses and scrub—or to desert.

- **This change** led to the extinction of many prehistoric herbivores, such as camel and horse species.

The first invertebrates

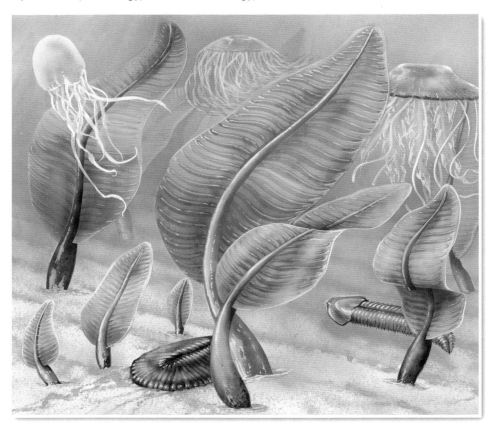

▲ Charnia *was a prehistoric animal that grew in feather-like colonies attached to the seabed, like living sea pens.* Charnia *fossils date to around 700 mya.*

- **An invertebrate** is an animal that does not have a spinal column. Invertebrates were the first animals to live on Earth, in the prehistoric seas.

- **The very first animal-like** organisms that fed on other organisms or organic matter were single-celled, and sometimes called protozoans.

- **Only prehistoric protozoans** with hard parts survive as fossils. The earliest fossils are around 700 million years old.

- **One of the earliest-known fossils** of a multi-celled animal is around 600 million years old. This is a creature called *Mawsonites*, which may have been a primitive jellyfish or worm.

- **Most of the earliest** invertebrate fossils are from extinct groups of animals.

- **Some of these animals** had segmented bodies that looked a bit like quilts.

- **One such invertebrate** is *Spriggina*, which is named after Reg Sprigg, a geologist. He discovered its fossilized remains near Ediacara in southern Australia in 1946.

- **Paleontologists** have unearthed the fossils of many other jellyfish-like invertebrates from Ediacara.

- **Another famous** invertebrate discovery was made by Roger Mason, an English schoolboy, in 1957. This was the fossil of *Charnia*, an animal that was similar to a living sea pen.

> ...FASCINATING FACT...
> *Spriggina* has a curved, shieldlike end to one part of its body. Some paleontologists think this was its head, while others think it was an anchor that secured it to the seabed.

More early invertebrates

- **The early, quilted invertebrates** were extinct by the beginning of the Cambrian Period (542–490 mya).

- **Paleontologists** regard their extinction as a loss that compares with the death of the dinosaurs at the end of the Cretaceous Period (around 65 mya).

- **Small, shelled invertebrates** emerged in the Early Cambrian Period.

- **These creatures included** the archaeocyathids, which had bodies that were like two cups, one inside the other.

- **Living animals** that most closely resemble archaeocyathids are sponges and corals.

- **Other small, shelled invertebrates** included animals such as *Tommotia* and *Latouchella*. They may have been early mollusks, the ancestors of snails and clams.

- *Tommotia* **and** *Latouchella* left behind fossils of their shells, which have strange-looking horns and tubes on the surface.

- **Other Early Cambrian invertebrates**, such as wormlike creatures, did not live in shells. Once predators began to appear, they would have made easy pickings.

- **Invertebrates** therefore evolved defenses against hunters, such as a tough exoskeleton (outer skeleton).

- **Another defense** was hiding. Many invertebrates, from worms to arthropods, began to burrow into the sea floor.

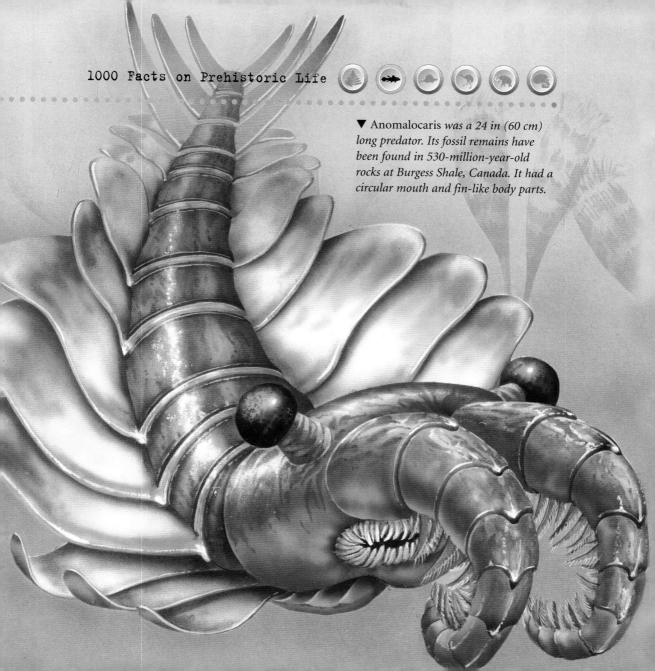

▼ Anomalocaris *was a 24 in (60 cm)* *long predator. Its fossil remains have* *been found in 530-million-year-old* *rocks at Burgess Shale, Canada. It had a* *circular mouth and fin-like body parts.*

Mollusks and graptolites

- **Modern mollusks** include gastropods (slugs, snails, and limpets), bivalves (clams, oysters, mussels, and cockles) and cephalopods (octopuses, squids, and cuttlefish).

- **Modern and prehistoric mollusks** represent one of the most diverse animal groups ever to have lived.

- **The first mollusks** were tiny—about the size of a pinhead. They appeared at the beginning of the Cambrian Period, about 542 mya.

- **The first cephalopod mollusks** emerged toward the end of the Cambrian Period, around 490 mya.

- **One early cephalod** was *Plectronoceras*, which had a hornshaped shell divided into different chambers.

- **Graptolites** had tentacles that they used to sieve food particles from water or the seabed.

- **Gastropod mollusks** (snails and slugs) were one of the first groups of animals to live on land.

- **Snails and slugs** are limited to where they can live on land as they require moist conditions.

- **Cephalopods** are the most highly developed of all mollusks. Squids and octopuses evolved big brains, good eyesight, tentacles, and beaklike jaws.

- **Graptolites are an extinct group** of mollusks that lived in stringlike communities, like lines. Graptolite means "written stone" because the fossils of the lines of these creatures resemble scrawled handwriting.

◀ *This snail is a mollusk. Its features include a muscular foot, a head with eyes and tentacles, and a shell. Today there are more than 100,000 living species of mollusks but many more times this number have lived in the past. They are very important as their shells make good fossils and some types evolved quickly, so their rapid changing shapes are used as "marker fossils" to date rocks.*

Ammonites

- **Ammonites** belong to the cephalopod group of mollusks.

- **They were once** widespread in the oceans, but, like the dinosaurs, died out at the end of the Cretaceous Period (about 65 mya).

- **The number** of ammonite fossils that have been found proves how plentiful these animals once were.

- **Ammonites** were predators and scavengers. They had very good vision, long seizing tentacles, and powerful mouths.

- **Their mouths** consisted of sharp beaks, poisonous glands, and a tooth-covered tongue.

- **Ammonites** had multi-chambered shells that contained gas and worked like flotation tanks, keeping the creatures afloat.

- *Stephanoceras* was an ammonite with a spiral, discshaped shell, 8 in (20 cm) across. It was very common in the seas of the Mesozoic Era (250–65 mya).

- **The closest living** relative of ammonites is *Nautilus*, a cephalopod that lives near the seabed and feeds on shrimps.

- **People once thought** that ammonite fossils were the fossils of curled-up snakes.

- **Builders** have traditionally set ammonite fossils into the walls of buildings for decoration.

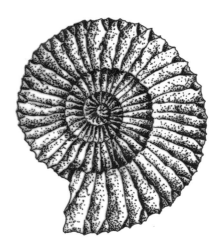

▶ *This shell protected the soft-bodied ammonite that lived inside it. Its tentacles would have poked out of the shell as it moved over the seabed, looking for food.*

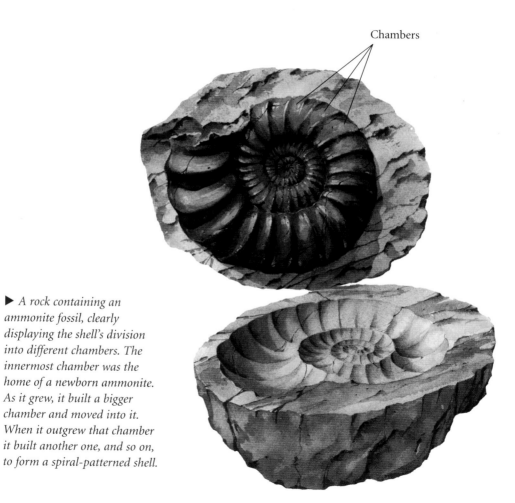

Chambers

▶ *A rock containing an ammonite fossil, clearly displaying the shell's division into different chambers. The innermost chamber was the home of a newborn ammonite. As it grew, it built a bigger chamber and moved into it. When it outgrew that chamber it built another one, and so on, to form a spiral-patterned shell.*

Worms

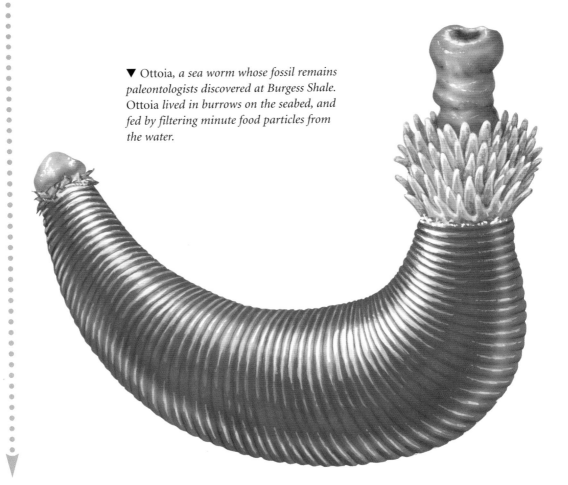

▼ Ottoia, *a sea worm whose fossil remains paleontologists discovered at Burgess Shale. Ottoia lived in burrows on the seabed, and fed by filtering minute food particles from the water.*

- **Worms** are invertebrates that usually have long, soft, slender bodies.

- **They were among** the earliest multi-celled animals to live in the prehistoric seas.

- **The soft bodies** of worms means that they do not make good fossils.

- **Much of our knowledge** of prehistoric worms comes from trace fossils, which include tracks, tunnels, and the impressions of their bodies in fine-grained rocks.

- **The tracks and trails** of early worms show that they were mobile creatures, which probably grazed the microbes that covered the sea floor.

- **The 530 million-year-old mudstone** deposits of the Burgess Shale in Canada contain the fossil impressions of worms.

- **Some of the Burgess Shale worms** like *Canadia* and *Burgessochaeta*, had thousands of hairlike bristles.

- *Canadia* is an annelid worm. In this type of worm, the body is divided into segments. Paleontologists think that millipedes and other arthropods evolved from annelids.

- **Some types of worms,** such as serpulid worms, secrete tubes, which they live in and which contain durable minerals.

- **Remains of serpulids' tubes** are quite common in rocks of the Mesozoic and Cenozoic Eras (250 mya to the present).

Trilobites

- **Trilobites** belonged to the invertebrate group called arthropods—animals with segmented bodies and hard outer skeletons.

- **Trilobite** means "three lobes". Trilobites' hard outer shells were divided into three parts.

- **The first trilobites** appeared about 530 mya. By 500 mya, they had developed into many different types.

- **Trilobites** had compound eyes, like insects' eyes, which could see in many different directions at once.

- **Some trilobites** could roll up into a ball, like some woodlice do today. This was a useful means of protection.

- **Trilobites** had long, thin, jointed legs. They moved quickly over the seabed or sediment covering it.

- **Trilobites** moulted by shedding their outer skeletons. Most trilobite fossils are the remains of these shed skeletons.

- **One of the largest trilobites** was *Isotelus*, which grew up to 17 in (44 cm) long.

- **Trilobites** could also be much smaller, such as *Conocoryphe,* which was about 1 in (2 cm) long.

- **Trilobites** became extinct around 250 mya—along with huge numbers of other marine animals.

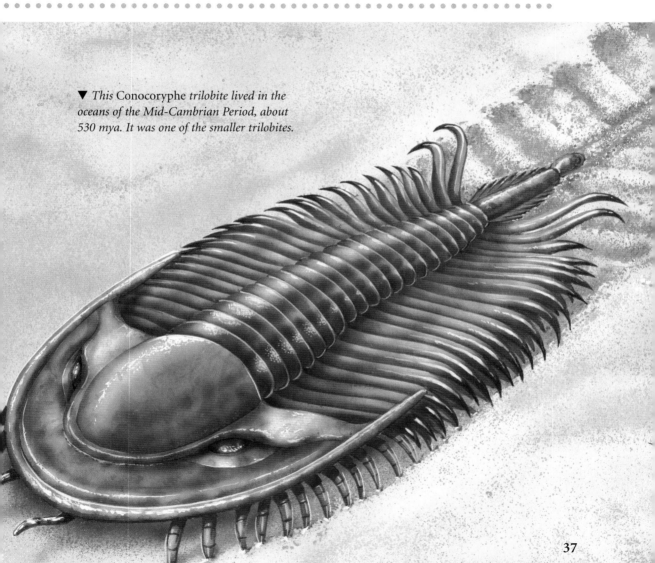

▼ *This* Conocoryphe *trilobite lived in the oceans of the Mid-Cambrian Period, about 530 mya. It was one of the smaller trilobites.*

Pterygotus

- *Pterygotus* was an enormous water scorpion that grew up to 8 ft (2.3 m) long.

- **Fossils of *Pterygotus*** have been found in rocks of the Silurian Period (435–410 mya).

- *Pterygotus* was a fearsome hunter, equipped with large eyes and long claws.

- **It had two huge claws** (called chelicerae) for grasping prey, two paddles for swimming, and eight legs for chasing victims over the seabed and digging them up from the sediment.

- *Pterygotus* belonged to the group of invertebrates known as eurypterids (water scorpions).

- **Eurypterids** lived between 490 and 250 mya.

- **Not all eurypterids** were giants—some were only 4 in (10 cm) long.

- **They were not** true scorpions, because their tail parts (called the opisthosoma) served as swimming paddles, not stinging weapons.

- *Pterygotus'* opisthosoma was long and ended in a flattened paddle. Paleontologists think it swam by beating this paddle up and down.

> **. . . FASCINATING FACT . . .**
> Dolphins swim by beating their tails up and
> down—which is how paleontologists think
> *Pterygotus* swam.

▼ Pterygotus, *which was bigger than a human, was the largest arthropod (an animal with a segmented body and a hard outer skeleton) ever to have lived.*

Insects, centipedes, and millipedes

- **Insects** evolved from sea-dwelling arthropods, such as trilobites. Like them, insects have segmented bodies, jointed legs, and exoskeletons (external skeletons).

- **The first land-living insects** appeared in the Devonian Period (410–355 mya).

- **Insects** made the transition to breathing air on land by developing small tubes called tracheae in their bodies.

- *Rhyniella* was the first known land insect. It was a springtail—an insect still alive today, which eats rotting plants and flips itself into the air if disturbed.

- *Latzelia* was an early centipede that lived on damp forest floors in the Carboniferous Period (355–298 mya).

- *Latzelia* had poisonous fangs, which it used to kill worms and other insects.

- **Insects** were the first animals to achieve flight. Early flying insects had stiff wings, which stuck out from their bodies—similar to dragonflies' wings.

- **The Cretaceous Period** (144–65 mya) saw a big rise in the number of flying insects, because of the emergence of flowering plants.

- **Many flowering plants** rely on flying insects to spread their pollen, while flying insects, such as bees, rely on flowers for food (nectar and pollen).

- **Beelike insects** date back to the Late Cretaceous Period, while modern bees first appeared around 30 mya.

▲ *The evolution of winged, pollinating insects, such as these honey bees, is closely linked to the evolution of flowering plants. Bees, as well as other flying insects, help these plants to spread by carrying pollen from the male part of one flower to the female part of another as they feed off nectar.*

Monster mini-beasts

- **The biggest insects** ever known lived in the forests of the Carboniferous Period (355–298 mya).

- **The size** of flying insects increased with the size of trees in the Carboniferous forests. One explanation for this is that they needed to fly higher to feed on the insects that lived in the tall trees.

- *Meganeura* was the largest-known winged insect, with a wingspan of up to 27.5 in (70 cm). It lived during the Late Carboniferous Period.

> ...FASCINATING FACT...
> Another huge Carboniferous dragonfly is known as the
> "Bolsover dragonfly," since its remains were discovered
> in Bolsover, England. It was the size of a seagull.

- **Like modern dragonflies**, *Meganeura* was unable to fold back its wings when it was resting.

- **The Carboniferous forests** were also home to enormous millipedes. They are known to paleontologists because of fossilized traces of their footprints. Some of these millipedes might have been as long as a human is tall.

- **Some millipedes** had poisonous fangs. A human-sized, poisonous millipede must have been a terrifying predator.

- **Mega-insects** did not live only in the Carboniferous Period. *Formicium giganteum* was a giant ant that lived about 45 mya.

- **Worker giant ants** grew up to 1 in (3 cm) long, but queens were nearly 2.4 in (6 cm,) with a wingspan of 5 in (13 cm)—bigger than some small birds!

- *Formicium giganteum's* closest living relative is the red wood ant.

◄ *Like this modern-day dragonfly,*
Meganeura *had large bulging eyes*
that allowed it to spot the movements
of potential prey. However, Meganeura
could be up to 15 times the size of a living
dragonfly, and had much stronger legs.

Pikaia

- *Pikaia* was a small, wormlike creature that is thought to be the ancestor of all backboned animals.

- **Its fossil remains** were found in the 530 million-year-old mudstone deposits of the Burgess Shale in Canada.

- *Pikaia* was the first-known chordate, a group of animals with a stiff supporting rod, called a notochord, along their back. All vertebrates belong to this group, as well as marine animals called tunicates and acraniates.

- *Pikaia* was 2 in (5 cm) long with a notochord (stiffening rod) running along its body—a kind of primitive spine that gave its body flexibility.

- **The notochord** also allowed the animal's simple muscles to work against it, and its body organs to hang from it.

- *Pikaia* is very similar to a modern creature called *Branchiostoma*, a small, seethrough creature that lives in the sand at the bottom of the sea.

- **As it lacks** a bony skeleton, a backbone, ribs, paired fins, and jaws, *Pikaia* is not really a fish.

- *Pikaia* is a more complex creature than many other animals found in the Burgess Shale. It suggests that other complex creatures must have lived before it, although there is (as yet) no fossil evidence for this.

- **The head** of the *Pikaia* was very primitive, with a pair of tentacles, a mouth, and a simple brain (a swelling of the nerve cord) for processing information.

- *Pikaia* swam in a zig-zag fashion, similar to a sea snake.

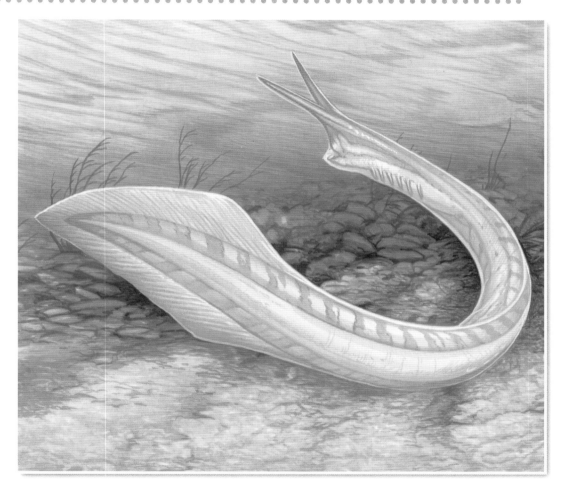

▲ Pikaia *looked a little like an eel with tail fins. The stiff rod that ran along its body developed, in later animals, into the backbone.*

Jawless fish

▲ *Early jawless fish, such as* Hemicyclaspis, *could swim much farther and quicker than most invertebrates. This meant they could more easily search for, and move to, new feeding areas.*

- **The first fish** appeared in the Late Cambrian Period, about 500 mya.

- **These fish** had permanently gaping mouths—as they had no jaws, they could not open and close their mouths.

- **Early fish** were called agnathans, which means "jawless."

- **Agnathans** ate by sieving plankton through their simple mouth opening, as well as scooping up algae on the seabed.

- **Among the oldest** complete agnathan fossils are *Arandaspis,* which comes from Australia, and *Sacabambaspis,* which comes from Bolivia.

- *Hemicyclaspis* was another agnathan. It was a very flat fish, with a broad head shield and a long tail.

- **Later jawless fish** had more streamlined, deeper bodies and eyes at the front of their heads. This suggests they were not restricted to the seabed.

- **Most jawless fish** died out by the end of the Devonian Period (around 350 mya).

- **Living relatives of agnathans** include lampreys and hagfish, which have soft bodies and look like eels. Like agnathans, they are also jawless.

> **...FASCINATING FACT...**
> *Hemicyclaspis* had eyes on top of its head. This
> suggests it lived on the seabed, and used its eyes to
> keep a lookout for predators above.

Jawed fish

- **The first jawed fish** emerged in the Early Silurian Period (about 430 mya).

- **Paleontologists** call jawed fish acanthodians, a name that comes from the Greek word *akantha,* meaning "thorn" or "spine."

- **Jaws and teeth** gave acanthodians a huge advantage over jawless fish—they could eat a greater variety of food and defend themselves more effectively.

- **Jaws and teeth** allowed acanthodians to become predators.

- **Acanthodians' jaws** evolved from structures called gill arches in the pharynx, the tube in vertebrates that runs from the mouth to the stomach.

- **Gill arches** are bony rods and muscles that surround the gills, the breathing organs of a fish.

- **As acanthodians developed** jaws, so they developed teeth, too.

- **The earliest** fish teeth were conelike shapes along the jaw, made out of bone and coated with hard enamel.

- **The teeth** of early acanthodians varied greatly. In some species they were sharp and spiky, in others they were like blades, while in others they resembled flat plates.

> ...FASCINATING FACT...
> Another difference between jawed and
> jawless fish was that jawed fish had a pair of
> nostrils, while jawless fishes only had one.

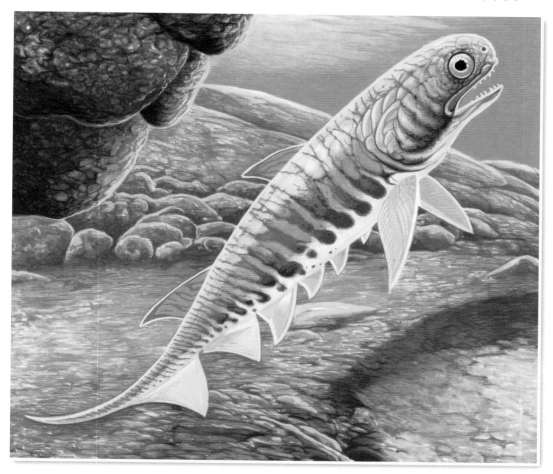

▲ A Climatius, *a type of acanthodian or jawed fish, that lived around 400 mya. Another name for acanthodians is "spiny sharks"—although they were not sharks, many had spines on the edges of their fins.*

49

Placoderms

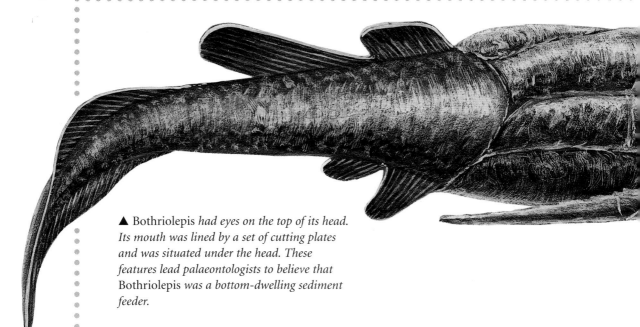

▲ Bothriolepis *had eyes on the top of its head. Its mouth was lined by a set of cutting plates and was situated under the head. These features lead palaeontologists to believe that* Bothriolepis *was a bottom-dwelling sediment feeder.*

- **Placoderms** were jawed fish that had bony plates covering the front part of the body.

- **They appeared** in the Late Silurian Period (about 415 mya) and were abundant in the oceans of the Devonian Period (410–355 mya).

- **Placoderm** means "plated skin." The plating provided placoderms—especially the smaller species—with protection against predators.

- **Most placoderms** were larger than acanthodians (the first jawed fish). They ranged in size from 12 in (30 cm) to 33 ft (10 m) in length.

  - **There were two groups** of placoderms—arthrodires and antiarchs.

    - **Arthrodires** had a ball-and-socket joint between the head and the front part of the body, which meant they could turn their head in many directions.

      - **Arthrodires** were predators, armed with powerful jaws and sharp teeth. They were very fast swimmers.

- **Antiarchs** were much smaller than arthrodires. Like arthrodires, antiarchs' head and the front part of its body were covered in bony plates.

- **Antiarchs** also had a pectoral (front end) fin connected to its head plates. Paleontologists think they might have used this fin as a leg, to help it move over the seabed.

> **...FASCINATING FACT...**
> *Dunkleosteus* was an arthrodire. It was a huge fish
> that could grow up to 33 ft (10 m) long. It was
> probably the biggest animal of its time, and is named
> after the man who discovered it, Dr David Dunkle.

Sharks

◄ Hybodus *was a blunt-headed prehistoric shark that lived between 250 and 125 mya, in the time of the dinosaurs. It looked quite similar to modern sharks, but had very different jaws.*

. . . FASCINATING FACT . . .
Prehistoric sharks' jaws were fixed to the side of their skull, while modern sharks' jaws hang beneath their braincase, which gives them a more powerful bite.

- **The earliest-known** shark fossils come from rock layers of the Early Devonian Period (410–355 mya).

- **Sharks** belong to the group known as cartilaginous fish, which also includes rays and skates. Their skeletons are made from cartilage, not bone.

- *Cladoselache* was a prehistoric shark, which could grow up to 7 ft (2 m) long.

- *Cladoselache* appears to have been quite similar to a modern shark—it had a streamlined body, a pair of dorsal (back) fins, and triangular-shaped pectoral (front end) fins.

- **Early sharks** hunted squid, small fish, and crustaceans.

- *Stethacanthus* was a prehistoric shark that looked nothing like a modern one. It had an anvil-shaped projection above its head, which was covered in teeth.

- *Stethacanthus* lived in the Carboniferous Period (355–298 mya).

- **Sharks** are at the top of the food chain in modern seas, but this was not the case during the Devonian Period.

- **Placoderms**, such as *Dunkleosteus*, dwarfed even the biggest sharks, and ate them for breakfast!

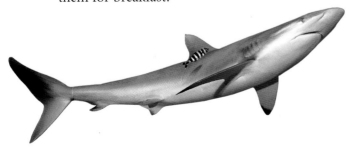

◄ *This modern blue shark, is a fast swimmer and a fierce hunter. The main features of sharks—from their tightly packed, needle-sharp teeth to their streamlined shape—have changed little over 400 million years.*

53

Bony fish

- **Bony fish** have internal skeletons and external scales made of bone.

- **They first appeared** in the Late Devonian Period (around 360 mya).

- **Bony fish** evolved into the most abundant and varied fish in the seas.

- **There are two types** of bony fish—ray-finned fish and lobe-finned fish.

- **There were plenty** of prehistoric lobe-finned fish, but only a few species survive today. They belong to one of two groups—lungfish or coelacanths.

- **Amphibians**—and, ultimately, reptiles, and mammals—evolved from lobe-finned fish.

- **Ray-finned fish** were so-called because of the bony rays that supported their fins. Most early ray-finned fish were small, ranging in size from about 2 in (5 cm) to 8 in (20 cm) long.

- *Rhadinichthys* **and** *Cheirolepis* were two early ray-finned fish. They were small predators, equipped with good swimming ability and snapping jaws.

- **Around 250 mya,** ray-finned fish lost many of the bony rays from their fins. The fins became less stiff and more flexible—and the fish became better swimmers.

- **New types of ray-finned fish,** called teleosts, also developed more symmetrical tails and thinner scales.

▶ *This modern-day coelacanth is a direct descendant of the lobe-finned bony fish that lived 350 mya. Coelacanths were thought to be extinct until a fisherman caught one off the coast of South Africa in 1938.*

Fins

- **The earliest fish** did not have fins. The first fish to have them were acanthodians (jawed fish).

- **Acanthodians** were the first fish predators. Fins gave them maneuverability, which they needed when chasing their prey.

- **Fins allow fish** to make quick or subtle changes in direction.

- **They also help fish** to stay afloat and counter the pull of gravity, since their bones and muscles are denser than water.

- **This explains why** most agnathans (jawless fish), which lacked fins, lived on the bottom of oceans—it meant they did not have to struggle against gravity.

- **Pectoral fins,** at the front end of a fish, help to keep it level and counteract its tendency to pitch forward at the front because of the weight of the head.

Dorsal fin

▶ *The skeleton of a great white shark. On its back is a large dorsal fin followed by a much smaller one. On its front are pairs of pectoral and pelvic fins. The caudal fin, the shark's tail, is used for propulsion and steering.*

Pectoral fin

- **Dorsal fins**, on a fish's back, and pelvic and anal fins at its rear, stop it from rolling over.

- **The first acanthodians** to have fins had a pair of dorsal fins, a single anal fin beneath the tail, and a varying number of pairs of fins on their undersides.

- **Later bony fish** developed pairs of fins that were borne by lobes, or projections, of bone and muscle. They were called lobe-finned fish.

- **The fins** of lobe-finned fishes evolved into the limbs of amphibians.

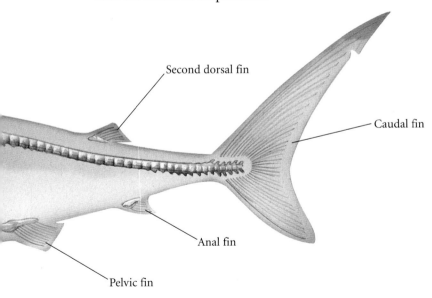

Second dorsal fin

Caudal fin

Anal fin

Pelvic fin

From fins to limbs

- **The first land-dwelling** backboned animals were called tetrapods. They needed legs to hold up their bodies and move around in search of water and food.

- **Tetrapods** evolved from lobe-finned fish, which had all the right body parts to develop arms and legs.

- **The fossil skeleton** of the lobe-finned fish *Eusthenopteron* shows that the organization of bones in its front and rear fins was similar to the arrangement of limbs in tetrapods.

- *Eusthenopteron* lived in shallow waters. It could use its fins as primitive legs and move over the land if the waters dried out.

- **Recent research suggests** that another lobe-finned fish, *Panderichthys*, could more effectively use its fins as limbs than *Eusthenopteron*. According to scientists, *Panderichthys* was more like a tetrapod than a fish.

- **The front fins** in lobe-finned fish connected to a shoulder girdle, while the rear fins connected to a hip girdle. These girdles connected to the backbone.

- **These hip and shoulder** connections meant that the limbs of future tetrapods were connected to a skeleton, which prevented the limbs from pressing against the inside of the body and damaging it.

> **...FASCINATING FACT...**
> Suitable fins were not the only feature that meant lobe-finned fish could evolve into land-dwelling animals. They also had lungs for breathing air!

- **The shoulder girdle** of lobe-finned fish also connected to their heads. Tetrapods, however, developed heads that were separated from their shoulders and joined instead by a neck.

- **Necks** were a great advantage to land-living animals. They could use them to bend down to feed, to reach up for food, and to turn around to see.

▲ Eusthenopteron *using its fins to move out of the water.* Eusthenopteron, *which means "good strong fin," was once thought to be the closest ancestor to tetrapods. However, paleontologists have recently discovered that another fish,* Panderichthys, *was an even closer relative.*

59

Tetrapods

- **Tetrapod** means "four-legged." All early tetrapods were amphibians as they were animals that could survive in water and on land.

- **The first tetrapods** emerged in the Late Devonian Period (about 360 mya).

- **They lived in warm**, shallow freshwater lakes and rivers. They developed limbs and lungs to cope with the waters drying out and this enabled them to move to new habitats.

- **The size of tetrapods** increased during the Carboniferous Period (355–298 mya). This may have been because there was more oxygen in the atmosphere, produced by the huge Carboniferous forests.

- **Tetrapods** adapting to the land had to face a range of challenges such as greater temperature variations than in water, and more ultraviolet radiation from the Sun.

▶ Eogyrinus
was an amphibious
tetrapod that lived around
310 mya. It grew up to 15 ft (4.5 m) long
and had a skull similar to a crocodile's and
a body similar to an eel's.

- **The early tetrapod**s were called labyrinthodonts, because of their labyrinth-like tooth structure. These animals include *Ichthyostega, Protogyrinus, Eogyrinus,* and *Diadectes.*

- *Diadectes* is the earliest-known plant-eating vertebrate. It was 10 ft (3 m) long and had small jaws with blunt teeth.

- **Modern amphibians** can be less than 4 in (10 cm) long, while early tetrapods could grow up to 7 ft (2 m).

- **Like their living descendants**—frogs and newts—early tetrapods laid eggs in water that hatched into tadpoles.

...FASCINATING FACT...
Some early tetrapods had seven digits (fingers and toes). Others had six or even eight. Eventually all tetrapods evolved to have five digits.

Breathing air

- **Fish** breathe oxygen in water through their gills. When a fish is out of the water, these gills collapse.

- **For creatures to adapt** to living on land, they had to develop air-breathing lungs.

- **Tetrapods** were not the first creatures to develop lungs—this step was taken by lobe-finned fish.

- **Lungfish** are lobe-fins that still exist today. They live in hot places and, when rivers dry out, bury themselves in mud and breathe through lungs.

- **Early tetrapods,** such as *Ichthyostega* and *Acanthostega,* had gills and lungs, which suggests they could breathe in both air and water.

- **Later tetrapods** breathed through gills when they were first born, but, like modern frogs and newts, their gills shrank when they got older and were replaced by lungs.

- **Modern amphibians** also take in oxygen through their skin, which is soft and moist.

- **Early tetrapods** had tougher skin, so were unable to breathe through it.

- **Breathing through skin** limits an animal's size, which is why modern amphibians are much smaller than many of their prehistoric ancestors.

> ...FASCINATING FACT...
> Animals could only evolve to live on land because of the work of plants over millions of years, producing oxygen that became part of Earth's atmosphere.

▼ *Prehistoric lungfish had lungs as well as gills. Like these modern lungfish, they were able to breathe air if the pools or rivers they lived in dried out.*

63

Acanthostega

▲ Acanthostega *may have evolved from lobe-finned fish such as* Eusthenopteron *and* Panderichthys. *It shared a number of features with these fish, including a similar set of gills and lungs, as well as tail fin and braincase.*

- *Acanthostega* was one of the earliest tetrapods. It had a fishlike body, which suggests it spent most of its life in water.

- **Its fossil remains** were found in rock strata dating from the Late Devonian Period (around 370 mya).

- *Acanthostega's* **body** was about 3.3 ft (1 m) long.

- **It had a wide tail**, which would have been useful for swimming but inconvenient for moving on land.

- **Its legs** were well-developed, however, with eight toes on the front feet and seven on the rear ones.

- **The number of toes** on its feet surprised paleontologists—they had previously thought all tetrapods had five toes.

- *Acanthostega's* **legs and toes** would have helped to give its body a thrusting motion when it swam. They would also help it to move through underwater plants at the bottom of rivers and lakes, in search of prey.

- *Acanthostega* had a flattened skull, and its eye sockets were placed close together on the top of its head.

- **A complete** but jumbled-up *Acanthostega* fossil was discovered in hard rock in Greenland. Paleontologists had to work very carefully to pry the fossil from the rock.

> ...FASCINATING FACT...
> *Acanthostega* had fishlike gills for breathing
> water as well as lungs for breathing air.

65

Ichthyostega

- *Ichthyostega* was another early tetrapod. Like *Acanthostega,* it was discovered in Greenland in rock that was 370 million years old.

- **Its body** was around 3.3 ft (1 m long). Paleontologists think it was probably covered in scales.

- *Ichthyostega* had a flat head, a long snout, large jaws, and teeth.

- **Its body** was barrel shaped. It had short, strong legs, and a fishlike tail.

- **This tetrapod** ate small fish and shellfish, but would have been prey for large fish.

- *Ichthyostega* had a skull that was completely solid apart from its eye sockets. This meant that there were no holes around which jaw muscles could attach.

- **Without proper jaw muscles,** *Ichthyostega* and other early tetrapods could do little more than snap their jaws open and shut.

- **Like** *Acanthostega*, *Ichthyostega* was more suited to swimming than walking. It used its legs for paddles, and its tail for manoeuvrability.

- *Ichthyostega* also used its limbs and feet for holding onto plants and digging for shellfish.

- *Ichthyostega* and *Acanthostega* show how animals were slowly adapting from a life in water to one on land.

▼ *Scientists think that* Ichthyostega's *shape and behavior were similar to that of seals. Like seals, it could probably tuck its limbs alongside its body when swimming. On land, it might have used its forelimbs to drag the rest of its body over the ground.*

Temnospondyls

- **Temnospondyls** were a group of tetrapods that emerged in the Carboniferous Period (355–298 mya). They were some of the biggest early tetrapods.

- *Gerrothorax* was a temnospondyl. It grew up to 3.3 ft (1 m) or more long and had a flattened body shape and a very wide, flat head, with eyes on top.

- *Gerrothorax* looked a little like an enormous tadpole. It probably spent most of its time in water rather than on land.

- **Its flat body shape** suited it to a life spent hunting by lying at the bottom of swampy waters and ambushing passing fish.

- **Other temnospondyls,** such as *Paracyclotosaurus* and *Cyclotosaurus,* had rounder bodies and thinner, sharper heads with powerful teeth and jaws—like an alligator's.

▶ Gerrothorax *was an aquatic temnospondyl of the Late Triassic Period (215–208 mya). Like most other temnospondyls, it was a predator.*

- *Gerrothorax*, *Paracyclotosaurus*, and *Cyclotosaurus* were all suited to watery habitats, but other temnospondyls show more adaptations for living on land.

- **One temnospondyl** that had a land-adapted body was the sturdily built *Cacops,* which grew to about 16 in (40 cm) long.

- **A much bigger** land-living temnospondyl was *Eryops,* which grew to about 7 ft (2 m) in length.

- **Temnospondyls** were the most successful land predators of their day.

- **They were all** destined for extinction, however. Temnospondyls were not the ancestors of reptiles—this role belonged to smaller tetrapods.

Lepospondyls

- **Lepospondyls** were another group of early tetrapods. Like temnospondyls, they first appeared between 350 and 300 mya.

- **Lepospondyls** were small animals, often about the size of modern-day newts 4–6 in (10–15 cm long).

- **Their backbones** differed from temnospondyls' backbones.

- **Lepospondyls** also had simpler teeth and fewer bones in their skulls than temnospondyls.

- *Diplocaulus* was a lepospondyl with strange wing shapes, which looked a bit like a boomerang, protruding from its skull.

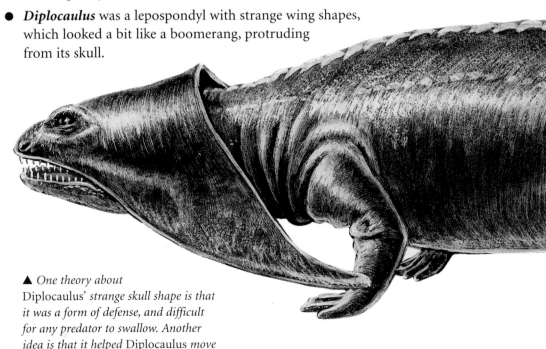

▲ *One theory about* Diplocaulus' *strange skull shape is that it was a form of defense, and difficult for any predator to swallow. Another idea is that it helped* Diplocaulus *move through the water, like a hydrofoil.*

- **It lived** in the Mid Permian Period (about 275 mya).
- **One *Diplocaulus* fossil** was found in Texas. It was 2.6 ft (0.8 m) long.
- ***Diplocaulus*** lived in freshwater streams. Its oddly shaped head probably increased its maneuverability in the water, like the rudder on a submarine.
- **Lepospondyls** were controversial creatures. Some paleontologists argue that they were the ancestors of modern amphibians.

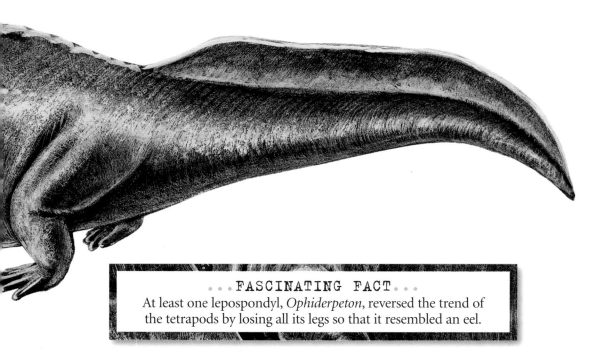

...FASCINATING FACT...
At least one lepospondyl, *Ophiderpeton*, reversed the trend of the tetrapods by losing all its legs so that it resembled an eel.

Frogs and salamanders

- **Modern amphibians,** such as frogs, toads, salamanders, and newts, all belong to the group called the lissamphibians.

- **Lissamphibians** evolved later than the early tetrapods, between the Late Carboniferous and Early Triassic Periods (300–240 mya).

▲ Triadobatrachus *was the earliest-known frog. Frogs and salamanders are descendants of a group of amphibious temnospondyls known as dissorophids.*

- *Triadobatrachus* lived in the Early Triassic Period, in Madagascar and was 4 in (10 cm) long.

- *Triadobatrachus* had a froglike skull. Compared to earlier amphibians, it had a shortened back, with fewer spinal bones, and a shortened tail.

- **Evolution** did not stop with *Triadobatrachus*—modern frogs have even fewer spinal bones and no tail at all.

- *Triadobatrachus'* hind legs were roughly the same size as its front legs. Again, this is different to modern frogs, which have long hind legs for hopping.

- *Karaurus* is the first known salamander. It lived in the Late Jurassic Period (around 150 mya) in Kazakhstan. It was 7.5 in (19 cm) long, with a broad skull.

- **More modern-looking frog** and salamander fossils have been discovered in Messel, Germany. They date from the Early Eocene Epoch (around 50 mya).

- **Some Messel frog fossils** have their legs bent, as if they were in mid-hop. There are even tadpole fossils from Messel.

> ...FASCINATING FACT...
> *Andrias scheuchzerii* was a salamander from the Miocene Epoch (24–5 mya). It was named after the Swiss scientist Johannes Scheuchzer, who discovered it in 1726.

First reptiles

- **Reptiles** evolved from amphibians during the Carboniferous Period (355–298 mya).

- **Unlike amphibians,** which usually live near and lay their eggs in water, reptiles are much more adapted for a life on land.

- **Compared to amphibians**, reptiles had better limbs for walking, a more effective circulatory system for moving blood around their bodies, and bigger brains.

- **They also had more powerful** jaw muscles than amphibians and would have been better predators. Early reptiles ate millipedes, spiders, and insects.

- **One of the earliest reptiles** was a small creature called *Hylonomus*, which lived in the Mid Carboniferous Period.

- *Hylonomus* lived in forests on the edges of lakes and rivers. Fossil remains of this reptile have been found inside the stumps of clubmoss trees.

- **Another early reptile** was *Paleothyris*. Like *Hylonomus*, it was about 8 in (20 cm) long, and had a smaller head than amphibians.

- **One animal** that represents a staging post between amphibians and reptiles is *Westlothiana lizziae,* which was discovered in Scotland in the 1980s.

- *Westlothiana lizziae* lived in the Early Carboniferous Period (about 340 mya).

- **At first** paleontologists thought that *Westlothiana lizziae* was the oldest reptile. But its backbone, head, and legs are closer to those of an amphibian.

▶ Hylonomus, *meaning "forest mouse," was one of the earliest reptiles. Fossil hunters discovered its remains in fossilized tree stumps at Joggins in Nova Scotia, Canada.*

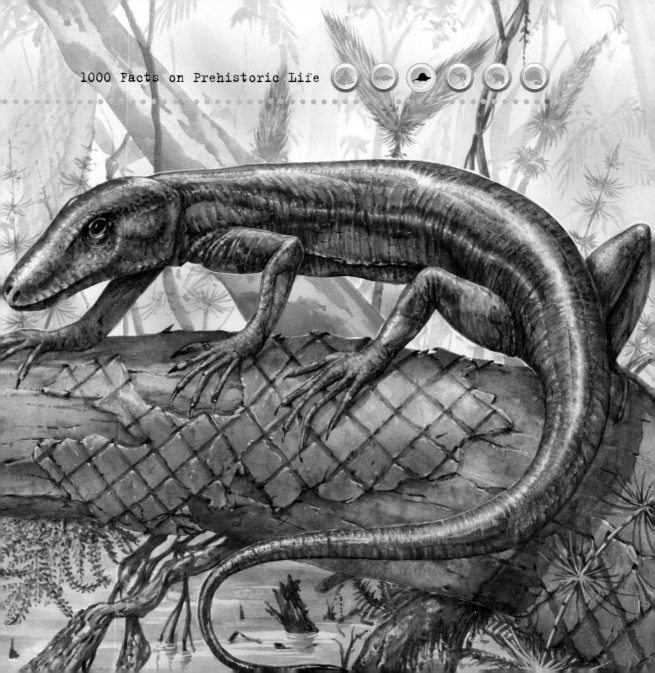

Eggs

- **Reptiles' eggs** are a major evolutionary advance over amphibians' eggs.

- **Early amphibians,** like modern ones, laid their eggs in water. This is because their eggs were covered in jelly (like modern frogspawn) and would dry out on land.

▲ *Amphibians lay their eggs, such as this frogspawn, in water.*

- **Reptiles** evolved eggs that were covered by a shell. This meant they could lay them on land and they would not dry out.

- **One advantage** of shelled eggs was that reptiles did not have to return to water to lay them.

- **Another advantage** was that reptiles could hide their eggs on land. Eggs laid in water are easy pickings for hungry animals.

- **Reptiles' embryos** complete all their growth phases inside eggs—when they hatch they look like miniature adults.

▶ *Reptiles broke the link between reproduction and water by laying hard-shelled eggs on land. This snake shell contains the developing young (the embryo), a food store (the yolk) and a protective liquid (the amniotic fluid).*

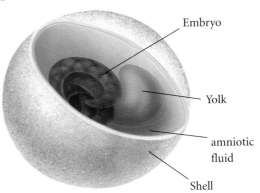

Embryo

Yolk

amniotic fluid

Shell

- **In contrast,** baby amphibians hatch out of their eggs as larvae, such as tadpoles. They live in water and breathe through gills before they develop lungs and can live on land.

- **Reptile shells** are hard, and protect the growing reptile embryos. They also provide them with food while they develop.

- **During the evolution** from amphibians to reptiles, some tetrapods laid jelly-covered eggs on land.

- **A number** of living amphibians lay jelly-covered eggs on land, including some tropical frogs and mountain salamanders.

▼ *A female snake protecting her eggs. Eggs laid on land are easier to protect than those laid in water.*

Skulls

- **The jaws of reptiles** are another feature that shows the evolutionary progression from amphibians.

- **Amphibians' jaws** are designed to snap but not to bite together tightly.

- **In contrast**, reptiles had more jaw muscles and could press their jaws together more firmly. This meant they could break insect body casings and chew through tough plant stems.

- **By the Late Carboniferous Period** (about 300 mya), reptiles developed openings in their skulls, behind the eye socket. These openings allowed room for more jaw muscles.

- **Four types of reptile skull** developed. Each belonged to a different type of reptile.

- **Anapsids** had no openings in their skull other than the eye sockets. Turtles and tortoises are anapsids.

- **Euryapsids** had one opening high up on either side of the skull. Sea reptiles, such as ichthyosaurs, were euryapsids, but this group has no surviving relatives.

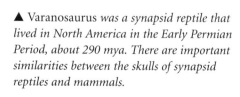

▲ Varanosaurus *was a synapsid reptile that lived in North America in the Early Permian Period, about 290 mya. There are important similarities between the skulls of synapsid reptiles and mammals.*

- **Synapsids** had one opening low down on either side of the skull. Mammals are descended from this group.

- **Diapsids** had two openings on either side of the skull. Dinosaurs and pterosaurs were diapsids; so too are birds and crocodiles.

...FASCINATING FACT...
Plants developed tough stems and leaves, spines, and poisons
to protect themselves frum hungry reptiles.

Synapsids

- **Synapsids** were a group of reptiles that had a pair of openings on their lower skull, behind the eye socket, onto which their jaw muscles attached.

- **Synapsids** are the ancestors of mammals, which explains why they are sometimes called "mammal-like reptiles."

- **These reptiles** first appeared in the Late Carboniferous Period (about 310 mya). They became the dominant land animals in the Permian and Triassic Periods (298–208 mya).

- **The first synapsids** are called pelycosaurs. They were large, heavy-bodied animals that walked a bit like modern-day crocodiles.

- **The fierce meateater** *Dimetrodon* and the plant-eating *Edaphosaurus*—both of which had long, fanlike spines on their backs—were pelycosaurs.

- **Later synapsids** are called therapsids. The earliest therapsids had bigger skulls and jaws than pelycosaurs, as well as longer legs and shorter tails.

- **Later therapsids** are divided into two subgroups—dicynodonts and cynodonts. Dicynodont means "two dog teeth"—cynodont means "dog tooth".

- **Dicynodonts** were herbivores. Most had round, hippopotamus-shaped bodies and beaks that they used to cut plant stems.

- **Cynodonts** were carnivores. They used different teeth in their mouth for different tasks—for stabbing, nipping, and chewing.

- **Cynodonts** were the most mammal-like of all reptiles. Some had whiskers

▶ Diictodon *was a mammal-like reptile that lived about 260 mya. A plant-eater and a burrower,* Diictodon *was an advanced form of a synapsid known as a dicynodont.*

Dimetrodon

- **Dimetrodon** was an early synapsid reptile called a pelycosaur. It was about 12 ft (3.5 m) long.

- **It was a carnivore,** and was one of the first land animals that could kill creatures its own size.

- **Dimetrodon** had a tall, skinny fin—a bit like a sail—running along its backbone. This fin was formed by a row of long spines that grew out of separate vertebrae.

- **Blood flowing** inside this sail would have been warmed by the early morning sun and carried to the rest of the body. The sail could also have radiated heat out, preventing overheating.

- **As a result**, *Dimetrodon* would warm up more quickly than other reptiles, so it could hunt them while they were still sluggish, cold or asleep.

- **Dimetrodon** had a deep skull and sharp, dagger-like teeth of different sizes. Its name means "two shapes of teeth."

- **In contrast with** other sail-backed pelycosaurs such as the herbivore *Edaphosaurus*, *Dimetrodon* had lightly built limbs and was a fairly fast mover.

- **Dimetrodon** was one of the dominant land predators between 280 and 260 mya.

- **After that time**, however, other reptiles, known as archosaurs, began to eclipse *Dimetrodon* because they were even bigger and better hunters.

- **Dimetrodon** was extinct by the beginning of the Triassic Period (about 250 mya).

◀ As well as allowing its body to quickly warm up or cool down, Dimetrodon's large fin might have helped it to attract mates or ward off rivals.

Moschops

- *Moschops* was a later synapsid reptile called a therapsid. It also belonged to a group of reptiles called dinocephalians (meaning "terrible heads"), because it had a very big skull.

- **It was a plant eater**, and was probably preyed upon by large flesh-eating dinocephalians, such as *Titanosuchus*.

- *Moschops* lived in the Permian Period (298–250 mya) in southern Africa.

- **It grew up to 16 ft (5 m) long**. It had a squat body and a short tail. Stocky limbs held it well off the ground.

- *Moschops* had many peglike, chisel-edged teeth, which were adapted for biting and uprooting plant matter.

- **Its back** sloped downward from the front, rather like a giraffe's.

- **It had enormous limb girdles** for both its front and rear legs, to support its heavy weight.

- *Moschops* had a high skull with an extremely thick bone on top, which it may have used to headbutt its rivals or enemies.

- **Its skull bones** became thicker as it got older. This thickening of the skull is called pachyostosis.

- **While *Moschops'* skull** was very big, its brain was not. "Bone head" might be a good nickname for it!

▼ *The bones on the top of Moschops'* skull could *be up to 4 in (10 cm) thick—enough to withstand the blows from head-butting rivals or enemies.*

Cynognathus

▼ Cynognathus *means "dog jaw." Like other synapsid reptiles, it had strong muscles for opening and closing its jaws, which made it a powerful killer.*

- **Cynognathus** was a therapsid reptile called a cynodont.

- **It lived** in the Early to Mid Triassic Period (250–220 mya).

- *Cynognathus* was the size of a large wolf, and weighed about 88–110 lb (40–50 kg).

- **Its skull** was about 16 in (40 cm) long, and its total body length was around 7 ft (2 m).

- **Like modern wolves,** *Cynognathus* was an active predator.

- *Cynognathus* had some very mammal-like features. Paleontologists think it may have been warm-blooded, may have had hair on its skin, and may have given birth to live young.

- **One of the many features** *Cynognathus* had in common with mammals was a bony palate that separated the mouth from the nasal cavity, and allowed it to breathe while it was eating.

- **Its teeth** were similar to a dog's. It had incisors (front teeth) for cutting, canines (teeth next to incisors) for piercing, and molars (cheek teeth) for slicing.

- **The legs** were designed for fast running—they were tucked underneath and close to its body unlike the legs of *Moschops,* which stuck out more at the sides.

- **Fossil skeletons of *Cynognathus*** have been found in South Africa. Paleontologists think that it favored hunting in dry, desert-like areas.

Crocodilians

- **The first crocodile-like reptiles** were called eosuchians, meaning "dawn crocodiles." They appeared in the Permian Period (298–250 mya).

- **The first true crocodiles** appeared at the end of the Triassic Period (about 215 mya). They were called protosuchians, and lived in pools and rivers.

- *Protosuchus* was, as its name suggests, a protosuchian. It had a short skull and sharp teeth, and would have looked quite like a modern crocodile.

- **Other early crocodiles**, such as *Terrestrisuchus*, looked less like modern crocodiles.

- *Terrestrisuchus* had a short body and long legs. Its name means "land crocodile," because paleontologists think it may have been more at home on land than in water.

▲ Fossils of Protosuchus, *meaning "first crocodile," have been discovered in Arizona, dating to around 200 mya. Although* Protosuchus *was similar to living crocodiles in many ways, its legs were much longer.*

> ...FASCINATING FACT...
> Modern crocodiles are living fossils. They look similar
> to the crocodiles that were alive 100 mya.

- **The next group** of crocodilians to evolve were the mesosuchians, which lived in the ocean.

- *Metriorhynchus* was a marine mesosuchian. It had flippers instead of limbs, and very sharp, fish-stabbing teeth. It lived in the Late Jurassic Period (around 150 mya).

- **One subgroup** of mesosuchians, the eusuchians, are the ancestors of modern crocodiles.

- *Deinosuchus* was an eusuchian. It was thought to be the largest-ever crocodile at 38 ft (11 m) long until a recent discovery of a *Sarchosuchus* fossil which is estimated to measure 52 ft (15 m).

Archosaurs

- **The archosaurs** (meaning "ruling reptiles") were a group of reptiles that came to dominate the land, seas, and skies in the Mesozoic Era (250–65 mya).

- **Archosaurs** included crocodilians, dinosaurs, and the flying reptiles called pterosaurs.

- **Archosaurs** are the ancestors of modern birds and crocodiles.

- **Archosaurs** were diapsid reptiles—they had two openings in the skull to which jaw muscles were attached, which meant their jaws were very powerful.

- **The first archosaurs** appeared in the Permian Period (around 255 mya). They would have looked quite like lizards, but with shorter bodies and longer legs and necks.

- **One early archosaur** was *Chasmatosaurus*. It had a large, heavy body, and probably spent most of its time hunting in rivers.

- *Lagosuchus* was another early archosaur. Some paleontologists think it might have been the direct ancestor of the dinosaurs.

- *Lagosuchus* was very small. It was about 12 in (30 cm) long and weighed about 3 oz (90 g). It had a slender body, and ran on its hind legs.

- **The name *Lagosuchus*** means "rabbit crocodile"—paleontologists think it may have moved like a rabbit by hopping.

> **...FASCINATING FACT...**
> Like many later dinosaurs, some early
> archosaurs were bipedal (two-legged walkers),
> leaving their arms free.

▲ Chasmatosaurus *was an early archosaur and a forerunner of the dinosaurs. It lived about 250 mya and grew up to 7 ft (2 m) long.*

Placodonts

- **After adapting** so well to life on land, some groups of reptiles evolved into water-dwelling creatures.

- **Placodonts** were early aquatic (water-living) reptiles. They lived in the Mid Triassic Period (about 240–220 mya).

- **The name placodont** means "plate tooth." These reptiles had large molars or cheek teeth that worked like large crushing plates.

- **Placodonts** appeared at about the same time as another group of aquatic reptiles, called nothosaurs.

- **They had shorter**, sturdier bodies than the nothosaurs but, like them, did not survive as a group for a very long time.

- *Placodus* was a placodont. It had a stocky body, stumpy limbs, and webbed toes for paddling. It may have had a fin on its tail.

- *Placodus* means "flat tooth." It probably used its flat teeth, which pointed outwards from its mouth, to pry shellfish off rocks.

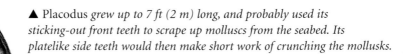

▲ Placodus *grew up to 7 ft (2 m) long, and probably used its sticking-out front teeth to scrape up molluscs from the seabed. Its platelike side teeth would then make short work of crunching the mollusks.*

- **Psephoderma** was a turtle-like placodont. Its body was covered in a shell, which in turn was covered by hard plates.

- **Psephoderma** also had a horny beak, like a turtle's, and paddle-shaped limbs.

- **Henodus** was another turtle-like placodont. It also had a beak, which it probably used to grab mollusks from the seabed.

Nothosaurs

- **Nothosaurs** were another group of reptiles that returned to live in the oceans.

- *Nothosaurus* was, as its name implies, a nothosaur. Its neck, tail, and body were all long and flexible.

- **Its total length** was about 10 ft (3 m) and its approximate weight was 176 lb (80 kg).

- **Impressions** left in some *Nothosaurus* fossils show that it had webs between its toes.

- *Nothosaurus'* **jaw** had many sharp, interlocking teeth, which would have crunched up the fish and shrimps on which it fed.

- *Ceresiosaurus* was another nothosaur. Paleontologists think it swam by swaying its body and tail from side to side, like a fish.

- *Ceresiosaurus* means "deadly lizard." It was bigger than *Nothosaurus* at 13 ft (4 m) in length and 198 lb (90 kg) in weight.

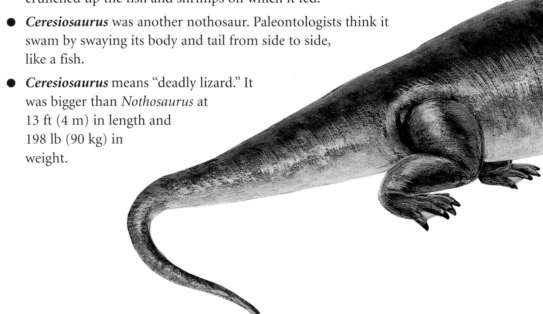

◄ Nothosaurus *was an aquatic reptile that could use its webbed feet to move over land. The long-necked nothosaurs were probably the ancestors of plesiosaurs, many of which also had long necks.*

● **Nothosaurs emerged** in the middle of the Triassic Period (250–208 mya), but were extinct by the end of it.

● **The place left by the extinct nothosaurs** was taken by the plesiosaurs—another group of marine reptiles, but ones that were better adapted to life in the oceans.

...FASCINATING FACT...
Nothosaurus had nostrils on the top of their snouts, which suggests that they came to the water's surface to breathe, like crocodiles.

95

Plesiosaurs

- **Plesiosaurs** were marine reptiles that were plentiful from the Late Triassic to the Late Cretaceous Periods (215–80 mya).

- **They were better suited** to a marine lifestyle than nothosaurs or placodonts. Their limbs were fully-developed paddles, which propelled their short bodies quickly through the water.

- **Many plesiosaurs** had a long, bendy neck, which ended in a small head with strong jaws and sharp teeth.

- **The diet** included fish, squid, and probably pterosaurs (flying reptiles), which flew above the water in search of food.

- **The first** Plesiosaurus fossil was discovered at Lyme Regis, on the south coast of England by Mary Anning in the early 19th century. The fossil, which is in the Natural History Museum, London, is 7.5 ft (2.3 m) long.

- *Plesiosaurus* was not a fast swimmer. It used its flipper-like limbs to move through the water but it had a weak tail that could not propel it forward very powerfully.

- *Elasmosaurus*, the longest plesiosaur, lived in the Cretaceous Period (144–65 mya). It grew up to 46 ft (14 m) long and weighed up to 3 tons.

- **One group of plesiosaurs** were known as pliosaurs. They had much shorter necks and much larger heads, with huge jaws and enormous teeth.

- **Research suggests** that plesiosaurs may have caught their prey with quick, darting head movements.

...**FASCINATING FACT**...
One large pliosaur was *Rhomaleosaurus*,
another was *Liopleurodon*. Both could
grow up to 49 ft (15 m) long.

▼ Plesiosaurus *was an early plesiosaur.*
It was about 15 ft (4.5 m) long—but
most of that length was its huge neck.

97

Ichthyosaurs

- **Ichthyosaurs looked similar** to sharks, which are fish, and to the later dolphins, which are mammals. When one type of animal evolves to look like another, scientists call it convergence.

- **Unlike plesiosaurs**, which relied on their paddles to propel them forwards, ichthyosaurs swayed their tails from side to side, like fish.

- **Hundreds of complete skeletons** of the ichthyosaur *Ichthyosaurus* have been discovered. This reptile could grow up to 7 ft (2 m) long, and weighed 198 lb (90 kg.)

- *Ichthyosaurus* had very large ear bones, which it may have used to pick up underwater vibrations caused by prey.

- **Some fossilized skeletons** of *Ichthyosaurus* and other ichthyosaurs have embryos (unborn infants) inside. This shows that ichthyosaurs gave birth to live young, as opposed to laying eggs.

- **One of the largest ichthyosaurs** was *Shonisaurus,* which was 49 ft (15 m) long and weighed 15 tons.

- **Ichthyosaurs** were plentiful in the Triassic and Jurassic Periods (250–144 mya), but became rarer in the Late Jurassic and in the Cretaceous Periods (144–65 mya).

- **Ichthyosaur** means "fish lizard."

- **Fossil-hunters** have found ichthyosaur remains all over the world—in North and South America, Europe, Russia, India, and Australia.

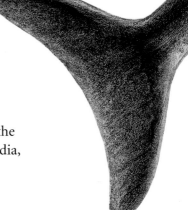

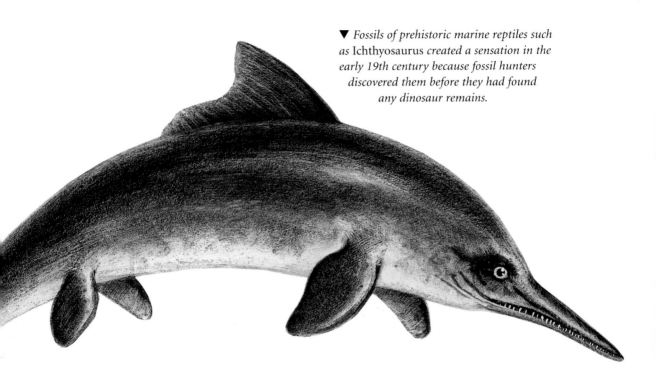

▼ Fossils of prehistoric marine reptiles such as Ichthyosaurus *created a sensation in the early 19th century because fossil hunters discovered them before they had found any dinosaur remains.*

...FASCINATING FACT...
The first *Ichthyosaurus* fossil was found in 1811 by the English fossil-hunter Mary Anning. It took seven years before scientists identified the skeleton as that of a reptile.

99

Mosasaurs

- **Mosasaurs** were another group of large sea reptiles. They appeared between 160 and 120 mya, at the time when ichthyosaurs were less common.

- **Mosasaurs** were diapsid reptiles, a group that included dinosaurs and pterosaurs. All other large sea reptiles belonged to another group, the euryapsids.

- **Unlike the other** giant prehistoric sea reptiles, mosasaurs have living relatives. These include monitor lizards, such as the Komodo dragon.

- **The best-known mosasaur** is *Mosasaurus,* which could be up to 30 ft (10 m) long and 10 tons in weight.

- **The huge jaws of *Mosasaurus*** were lined with cone-shaped teeth, each of which had different cutting and crushing edges. They were the most advanced teeth of any marine reptile.

- **So distinctive** are *Mosasaurus'* teeth that paleontologists have identified its tooth marks on the fossils of other animals, in particular the giant turtle *Allopleuron.*

- **The jaws of a *Mosasaurus*** were discovered in a limestone mine in Maastricht, in the Netherlands, in 1780. The fossil disappeared in 1795 when the French invaded Maastricht, but later turned up in Paris.

- **At first,** scientists thought the jaws belonged either to a prehistoric whale or a crocodile, until they decided they were a giant lizard's.

- ***Mosasaurus*** means " from the River Meuse," because it was discovered in Maastricht in the Netherlands, through which the River Meuse flows.

- **In 1998**, more than 200 years after the discovery of the first Mosasaurus fossil, paleontologists discovered the remains of another Mosasaurus in the same location—the St. Pietersburg quarry in Maastricht.

▼ Mosasaurus *was a fast swimmer. It had an enormous tail and paddle-shaped limbs, which it probably used as rudders.*

Rhamphorhynchoids

▶ Dimorphodon *had a wingspan of between 4–8 ft (1.2–2.5 m). Paleontologists think that it lived and hunted along seashores and rivers.*

- **The earliest pterosaurs** (flying reptiles) were the rhamphorhynchoids. They first appeared in the Late Triassic Period (around 220 mya).

- **Rhamphorhynchoids** had long tails that ended in a diamond-shaped vane, like a rudder.

- **Their tails** gave them stability in flight, which meant they could soar and swoop effectively.

- **One of the first rhamphorhynchoids**—and first flying vertebrates—was *Peteinosaurus*.

- **Well-preserved fossils** of *Peteinosaurus* have been found near Bergamo in Italy.

- **They reveal Peteinosaurus'** sharp, conelike teeth, and suggest it ate insects, which it caught in the air.

- **In contrast**, another early rhamphorhynchoid, *Eudimorphodon*, had fangs at the front of its mouth and smaller spiked ones behind. This suggests that it ate fish.

- ***Dimorphodon*** was a later rhamphorhynchoid from the Early Jurassic Period (208–180 mya). It had a huge head that looked a bit like a puffin's.

- ***Rhamphorhynchus*** was one of the last rhamphorhynchoids, appearing in the Late Jurassic Period (about 160 mya).

▶ Rhamphorhynchus *had long, sharp jaws that it used to spear fish.*

...**FASCINATING FACT**...
Fossil-hunters have found *Rhamphorhynchus* fossils alongside those of the early bird *Archaeopteryx*, in Solnhofen, Germany.

103

Pterodactyls

- **Pterodactyls** are a later group of pterosaurs (flying reptiles) than the rhamphorhynchoids.

- **They lived** in the Late Jurassic through to the Late Cretaceous Periods (160–65 mya).

- **Pterodactyls** lacked the long, stabilizing tail of rhamphorhynchoids, but were more effective fliers, as they were able to make quicker turns in the air.

- **They were also** much lighter than rhamphorhynchoids, because their bones were hollow.

- **The pterodactyl** *Pterodactylus* and the rhamphorhynchoid *Rhamphorhynchus* were roughly the same size, but *Pterodactylus* weighed between 2.2–11 lb (1–5 kg), while *Rhamphorhynchus* weighed 22 lb (10 kg).

- **Some of the largest pterodactyls,** such as *Pteranodon,* appeared in the Late Cretaceous Period and had a wingspan of 23 ft (7 m).

▶ Pterodactylus *was a small pterosaur that lived next to the ocean. It fed on fish and shellfish.*

- **Unlike earlier flying reptiles**, *Pteranodon* had no teeth. Instead, it used its long, thin beak to scoop up fish.

- *Pteranodon* also had a pelican-like pouch at the bottom of its mouth—it probably used this to store fish before swallowing them.

- *Pteranodon* weighed about 35 lb (16 kg). This was heavier than earlier pterodactyls, and suggests it was probably a glider rather than an active flyer.

- *Pteranodon* had a long crest on its head, which may have worked as a rudder during flight.

▼ Pteranodon, *meaning "wings and no teeth," was once thought to be the largest ever flying reptile—until the discovery of* Quetzalcoatlus *(see pages 106–107) in the 1970s.*

105

Quetzalcoatlus

- *Quetzalcoatlus* was the largest known flying animal of any kind ever to have lived.

- **It had a wingspan of 49 ft (15 m)**—the size of a small aeroplane!

- **It was also the heaviest** flying reptile, weighing 189.5 lb (86 kg). Its bulk suggests that it was not a brilliant flyer, and instead glided as much as possible.

- **Its name** comes from an Aztec word meaning 'feathered serpent'. Quetzalcoatl was the Aztec god of death and resurrection.

- *Quetzalcoatlus* had long, narrow wings, jaws without teeth, and a long, stiff neck.

- **Paleontologists** were amazed when they discovered the fossilized bones of *Quetzalcoatlus*—they did not think a flying creature could be that large.

- **The discovery** of these bones in inland areas, not coastal regions like those of other flying reptiles, suggests *Quetzalcoatlus* may have soared above deserts, like a vulture.

- **Some paleontologists** say that *Quetzalcoatlus* was nothing like a vulture because its beak was not designed for ripping at the bodies of dead animals.

- **Another puzzle** for paleontologists and mathematicians is how *Quetzalcoatlus* could lift itself off the ground to fly.

...FASCINATING FACT...
A student, Douglas Lawson, discovered *Quetzalcoatlus'*
bones in the Big Bend National Park, Texas, in 1971.

▼ Quetzalcoatlus *belonged to a family of*
pterosaurs called the azhdarchids, which
had giant wingspans, long necks, and
toothless beaks. The name "azhdarchid"
comes from the Uzbek word for a dragon.

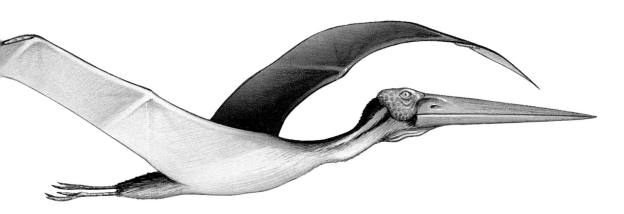

Flight

- **Pterosaurs** (flying reptiles) evolved wings that consisted of a stretched membrane (a piece of thin skin).

- **The fourth finger** of flying reptiles was extremely long, and held up the wing membrane.

- **As well as the main** wing membrane, flying reptiles also had an additional flap of skin, stretched between the shoulder and wrist, that gave added stability during flight.

- **Over time**, the forelimbs of birds became elongated and developed into wings.

- **They also** developed feathers, which possibly evolved from the scales of their reptile ancestors.

- **Flying birds** have asymmetrical feathers, which have longer barbs on one side of the shaft than on the other. This helps to lift them up and allows them to move in the air. Flightless birds have symmetrical feathers—in which the shaft runs down the middle—which is why they cannot fly.

- **One theory** of how birds and reptiles developed flight is that as they ran along the ground, they flapped their arms to give them stability. Over time, these arms developed into wings.

- **Another theory** is that, before they could fly, some reptiles and birds glided from tree to tree in search of food. They then developed wings and flight.

- **The feathered wings** of birds survive injuries better than the more fragile skin wings of flying reptiles could have done. This may suggest why birds have outlived pterosaurs.

....FASCINATING FACT....

The reason why paleontologists are confident that *Archaeopteryx*, the first known bird, could fly is because it had asymmetrical feathers.

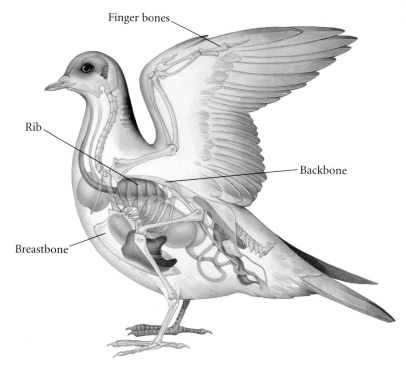

Finger bones

Rib

Backbone

Breastbone

▲ *Birds' skeletons, such as this modern-day pigeon's, are built for flight. The bones are lightweight and often hollow; the finger bones in the wing are joined to provide greater strength; and the ribs, backbone, and breastbone form a secure cage that supports powerful wings.*

109

Archaeopteryx

- **_Archaeopteryx,_** from two Greek words meaning "ancient wing," is the earliest known flying bird.

- **It lived** in the Late Jurassic Period (159–144 mya).

▼ Archaeopteryx *is the first known flying bird, but it would not have been a very efficient flyer because of its primitive skeleton and long tail.*

> ...FASCINATING FACT...
> The chick of the hoatzin bird, which lives in Venezuela and
> Guyana, has claws on each wing that are very similar to
> *Archaeopteryx's*. It uses them to climb and cling onto trees.

- ***Archaeopteryx*** was roughly the size of a magpie—it would have weighed about 9.5 oz (270 g) and had a wingspan of approximately 24 in (60 cm).

- **Probably eight identified** *Archaeopteryx* fossils have been found, ranging from almost a whole skeleton to just one feather, all of them preserved in limestone, in Solnhofen, southern Germany.

  - **The fossils reveal** that *Archaeopteryx* had feathers and that, like modern birds, they were asymmetrical—one side was thicker than the other.

    - ***Archaeopteryx*** was therefore capable of flight, but could not fly long distances because it lacked a suitable skeleton.

    - **Like carnivorous dinosaurs**, *Archaeopteryx* had jaws with teeth, and forelimbs (arms) that had separate fingers with claws.

    - ***Archaeopteryx*** looks so similar to a small dinosaur that one museum labelled its *Archaeopteryx* fossil as such for decades—until someone realized it had feathers.

    - ***Archaeopteryx*** was a tree-dwelling creature. The big toe at the end of its hind legs pointed backward, allowing it to grip branches.

Confuciusornis

- *Confuciusornis* was the first-known bird to have a true birdlike beak.

- **It lived in** the Late Jurassic to Early Cretaceous Periods (around 150–120 mya).

- **Unlike the slightly older** *Archaeopteryx,* which had a mouth filled with teeth, *Confuciusornis,* had a toothless beak, like modern birds.

- **This beak** had an upward curve—a fact that has led paleontologists to argue about this bird's diet. Some think it ate seeds and others that it hunted fish.

- *Confuciusornis* was approximately 24 in (60 cm) long.

- **It had** lightweight bones, a deep chest, and a short, rudder-like tail. All of this means it was probably a better flyer than *Archaeopteryx.*

- **Like** *Archaeopteryx*, it had a backward-pointing big toe on its hind feet, which suggests it lived in trees.

- **The remains** of *Confuciusornis* were discovered at the Liaoning Fossil Beds, in northeast China, in the mid 1990s.

- **The Liaoning Fossil Beds** were the site of a prehistoric lake. Fossil-hunters have found so many *Confuciusornis* fossils at this site that the bird probably lived in large colonies on the lakeshore.

- *Confuciusornis* means "Confucius bird." It is named after the ancient Chinese philosopher Confucius.

▼ *A male* Confuciusornis. *Scientists think that males had long tail feathers, but females had much shorter tails.*

Terror birds

- **After the dinosaurs** became extinct (about 65 mya), huge flightless birds—known as terror birds—seized the opportunity to become the dominant predators of their day.

- *Gastornis* was one such terror bird. It had an enormous head and powerful legs, like those of its dinosaur ancestors, so it could outrun its prey.

- **Some experts** believe that *Gastornis* is the ancestor of ducks, geese, and other related birds.

- **Even though these birds** could be huge, they were also light-footed, quick runners. This is because, like all birds, they had hollow bones.

- **The diets** of terror birds included small and medium-sized mammals, such as prehistoric rodents and horses.

- **During the Late Eocene** and Oligocene Epochs (40–24 mya), the big carnivorous mammals became more powerful and better hunters and so more dominant, taking over.

▶ Gastornis *was about 6.5 ft (2 m) tall, with a head the size of a horse's. Around 50 mya it was one of the top hunters in Europe and North America.*

114

> ...**FASCINATING FACT**...
> Unlike other flightless birds, *Titanis* had clawed fingers at the end
> of its forelimbs. It probably used these fingers for seizing its prey.

- **However, in South America,** which was cut off from North America and the rest of the world for much of the Tertiary Period (65–1.6 mya), terror birds managed to stay dominant for longer.

- **One South American** terror bird was *Phorusrhacus,* which grew up to 5 ft (1.5 m) tall.

- ***Titanis*** was another South American terror bird, and the biggest of all—it was 8 ft (2.5 m) tall and weighed 330 lb (150 kg.)

▶ Phorusrhacus *probably hunted on open grasslands, seizing goat-sized mammals with its huge beak.*

115

Other flightless birds

- **Most prehistoric** flightless birds were giants, but not all of them were terror birds.

- *Shuvuuia,* which lived about 80 mya, was an early, flightless bird. Like the terror birds, it was very large.

- *Shuvuuia* was about 3.3 ft (1 m) high. It probably fed on insects and small reptiles.

- **The name *Shuvuuia*** comes from the Mongolian word for "bird." It lived on the plains of Central Asia and had the long, thin legs of a fast runner.

- **For a long time,** paleontologists thought that *Shuvuuia* was a reptile, but in fact its skull is much more similar to a modern bird's than a reptile's.

- **Much later giant** birds grew to incredible sizes. *Dinornis,* for instance, was the tallest flightless bird ever at 11.5 ft (3.5 m) tall.

- *Dinornis* lived in New Zealand. It first appeared about 2 mya and survived until 300 years ago!

- **At 992 lb (450 kg),** *Aepyornis* was the heaviest bird ever to have lived. It lived on the island of Madagascar between 2 million and 500 years ago.

- **Both *Dinornis* and *Aepyornis*** were herbivores. Their diet consisted of seeds and fruit.

> ...FASCINATING FACT...
> *Dinornis* was a type of moa bird. The
> only survivor of this group is the kiwi.

Ostrich

Emu

Rhea

Cassowary

Bennet's
cassowary

Kiwi

▲ *These living flightless birds are descendants of prehistoric flightless birds. The collective name for flightless birds is ratites, from the Latin* ratis *meaning "raft." Unlike flying birds, ratites have flat, raftlike breastbones that cannot support the muscles needed for flight.*

Water birds

- *Ichthyornis* was a prehistoric seagull, which first appeared in the Late Cretaceous Period (85–65 mya).

- **It was similar in size** to a modern seagull, but had a much larger head and a beak full of very sharp teeth.

- *Presbyornis* was a prehistoric duck. Like *Ichthyornis,* it evolved in the Late Cretaceous Period and was abundant in the Early Tertiary Period (65–40 mya).

- *Presbyornis* was much bigger than a modern duck—it stood between 1.6–5 ft (0.5 m–1.5 m) tall.

- **It had much longer legs** than its modern relative and so may have been a wading bird rather than a diving bird.

- *Presbyornis* lived in large flocks on lake shores, like modern flamingos.

- *Osteodontornis* was a huge flying bird, with a wingspan up to 17 ft (5.2 m) across.

- **It lived in the Miocene Epoch** (24–5 mya), and would have flown over the North Pacific Ocean.

- *Osteodontornis* had a long bill, lined with toothlike bony spikes. Its diet probably included squid, seized from the surface of the ocean.

> . . . **FASCINATING FACT** . . .
> The skull of *Presbyornis* most closely resembles that
> of the living Australian duck *Stictonetta*.

118

▶ Some experts believe that Palaelodus *was a prehistoric flamingo that lived in France about 26 mya.*

Land birds

- **Land birds** are flying birds that fly in the skies over land and hunt or feed on the ground, unlike water birds.

- **Fossils** of prehistoric land birds are rare because their bones were light and would not have fossilized well.

◀ *No one knows for certain when parrots first evolved, but fossils date back to at least 20 mya. Some bird experts think that parrots were once much more plentiful than they are today.*

. . . **FASCINATING FACT** . . .
Neocathartes was an early vulture-like bird. There are similarities between its skeleton and that of storks, which suggests vultures and storks are closely related.

- **As a result**, there are big gaps in paleontologists' knowledge of the evolution of many species of birds. However, there are some early land birds they do know about.

- *Archaeopsittacus* was an early parrot of the Late Oligocene Epoch (28–24 mya).

- *Ogygoptynx* was the first-known owl. It lived in the Palaeocene Epoch (65–58 mya).

- *Aegialornis* was an early swiftlike bird, which lived in the Eocene and Oligocene Epochs (58–24 mya). It may be the ancestor of swifts and hummingbirds.

- *Gallinuloides* was an early member of the chicken family. *Gallinuloides* fossils have been found in Wyoming, in rock strata of the Eocene Epoch (58–37 mya).

- **The earliest-known vultures** lived in the Palaeocene Epoch (65–58 mya).

- **The earliest-known hawks**, cranes, bustards, cuckoos, and songbirds lived in the Eocene Epoch.

▶ *This vulture's earliest ancestors were the very first birds of prey. Scientists think that* Lithornis, *a bird of prey that lived around 65 mya, was a type of vulture.*

Argentavis

- *Argentavis* was an enormous bird of prey—the largest one ever discovered.

- **Its wingspan** was more than 23 ft (7 m) across, which is double the size of the largest modern living bird, the wandering albatross.

- **Individual** *Argentavis* feathers were up to 5 ft (1.5 m) long!

- *Argentavis* lived between 8 and 6 mya.

- **It looked similar** to a modern vulture, and may have had a similar scavenging lifestyle.

- **Its huge size** and weight (up to 176 lb/80 kg) suggests that it was more of a glider than an active flier.

- *Argentavis* was possibly bald-headed, with a ruff of feathers around its neck, much like a modern vulture or a condor.

- **It had a large**, hooked beak, which was probably more effective at grabbing hold of prey than its feet.

- **Argentavis** means "bird of Argentina" and it is so-called because its remains were first discovered there.

- **Argentavis** belonged to a family of extinct flying birds called teratorns.

◀ The colossal Argentavis, *whose fossils were discovered in 1979, is an ancestor of North American turkey vultures.*

Rise of the mammals

- **The earliest mammals** were small, shrewlike creatures that appeared in the Late Triassic Period (220–208 mya).

- **After their initial emergence**, mammals developed little in the two periods following the Triassic, Jurassic, and Cretaceous Periods (208–65 mya).

- **This is because dinosaurs** dominated the land at this time. Mammals had to remain small and hidden to avoid becoming dinner!

- **It was only after dinosaurs** became extinct around 65 mya, that mammals started to evolve into larger and more varied forms.

▼ *This timeline shows a selection of mammals from the various main groups like whales, primates, horses, and elephants. Many kinds of mammals came and went during prehistory, and the ones that are alive today are a relatively limited selection of all the mammals that have ever existed on Earth.*

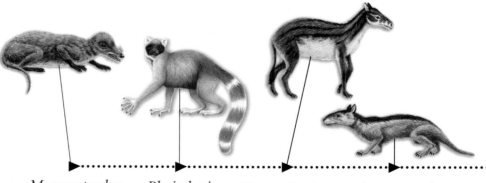

Megazostrodon
220 mya

Plesiadapis
60 mya

Hyracotherium
60–50 mya

Icaronycteris
55–45 mya

- **Mammals** (and birds) have bigger brains than reptiles, and are also warm-blooded.

- **These abilities** meant that mammals could be adaptable—something that ensured their success in the changing climates of the Tertiary and Quaternary Periods (65 mya to the present).

- **The rise of mammals** to the top was not instant—during the Early Tertiary Period, (65–58 mya), the major killers were the giant flightless terror birds.

- **During the Eocene Epoch**, (58–37 mya), mammals became the most dominant animals on land.

- **Eocene mammals** also took to the air in the form of bats—and the oceans in the form of whales—and later, dolphins, and seals.

- **Mammals have been**, and still are, the most adaptable of all backboned animals.

Basilosaurus
40 mya

Paraceratherium
30 mya

Smilodon
1 mya

Wooly Mammoth
120,000 years ago

125

Early mammals

- *Megazostrodon* was one of the first true mammals. It appeared at the end of the Triassic Period (about 220 mya).

- **It was a shrewlike insectivore** (insect-eater) and about 5 in (12 cm) long. It had a long body that was low to the ground and long limbs that it held out to the side in a squatting position.

- *Eozostrodon* was another very early mammal, which emerged about the same time as *Megazostrodon*.

- **It had true mammalian teeth**, including two different sorts of cheek teeth—premolars and molars—which were replaced only once during its lifetime.

- **Its sharp teeth** suggest it was a meat eater, and its large eyes suggest that it hunted at night.

- **A further early mammal** was *Morganucodon*. It too had premolars and molars and chewed its food in a roundabout motion, rather than the up-down motion of reptiles.

- *Sinoconodon* was yet another early mammal that lived in the Early Jurassic Period (about 200 mya). It was probably covered in fur.

- **These early mammals** also had three middle ear bones, which made their hearing more sensitive than reptiles.

▲ *Like other small, early mammals,* Megazostrodon *was probably a nocturnal animal, coming out to hunt at night.*

- **They also had whiskers**, which suggests they had fur, which in turn suggests they were warm-blooded.

- **All true mammals** are warm-blooded, which means they maintain a constant body temperature. Fur helps mammals to keep warm when it is cold—at night, for instance.

127

Offspring

- **Mammals** developed a very different way of producing young, compared to reptiles and birds, which both lay eggs.

- **Instead, most mammals** are viviparous, which means they give birth to live young.

- **One unusual group of mammals**, the monotremes, defy this rule by laying eggs. There are five surviving monotremes—the duck-billed platypus and four species of echidna.

▼ *All mammal offspring such as these lambs, feed on their mother's milk, which contains a rich source of nutrients to help them to grow quickly.*

- **After the young** of mammals are born, their mothers feed them milk, produced in their mammary glands.

- **The word "mammal"** comes from the mammary glands—the part of female mammals' bodies that secretes milk.

- **The first mammals**, such as *Megazostrodon, Eozostrodon,* and *Morganucodon* grew a single set of milk teeth, which suggests that the young fed on breast milk.

- **Milk teeth** are temporary teeth that grow with the nutrients provided by milk, and prepare the jaw for later teeth.

- **Mammals** can be divided into three groups depending on how they rear their young—placentals, marsupials and monotremes.

- **In placental mammals**, the offspring stays inside its mother's body, in the womb, until it is a fully developed baby —at which point it is born.

- **Marsupial mammals** give birth to their offspring at a much earlier stage. The tiny infants then develop fully in their mothers' pouch, called a marsupium (see pages 152–153).

◄ *Marsupial mammals, such as this kangaroo and its joey (infant), give birth at an earlier stage than other mammals.*

Rodents

- **In terms of their numbers**, variety, and distribution, rodents are the most successful mammals that have ever lived.

- **Squirrels**, rats, guinea pigs, beavers, porcupines, voles, gophers, and mice are all types of rodent.

- **Rodents** have been—and still are—so successful because they are small, fast-breeding, and able to digest all kinds of foods, including substances as hard as wood.

- **The first-known rodent** was *Paramys,* which appeared about 60 mya.

- *Paramys* was a squirrel-like rodent that could climb trees. It was 24 in (60 cm) long, and had a long, slightly bushy tail.

- **Modern squirrels** evolved from *Paramys* around 38 mya. These mammals have one of the longest ancestries that we know of.

- **Another early rodent** was *Epigaulus,* which was a gopher with two horns.

- *Epigaulus* was 10 in (26 cm) long and lived in North America in the Miocene Epoch (24–5 mya). It probably used its horns for defense or digging up roots.

- **Prehistoric rodents** could be massive. *Castoroides* was an early beaver that was over 7 ft (2 m) long—almost the size of a black bear.

> ...FASCINATING FACT...
> Rabbits and hares are descended from rodents.
> Modern hares first appeared around 5 mya.

▼ Platypittamys *was a prehistoric, ratlike rodent. Rodents became plentiful during the Oligocene Epoch (37–24 mya).*

Carnivores

- **The first carnivorous mammals** were the creodonts, which ranged in size from the cat-like *Oxyaena* to the wolflike *Mesonyx*.

- **In the Late Eocene Epoch** (around 40 mya) large hoofed carnivores began to appear, such as *Andrewsarchus*.

- **Modern carnivores** are descended from a seperate group called miacids.

- **Modern carnivores** belong to the order Carnivora. This order had two subgroups—the fissipeds, which include the cat and dog families and the pinnipeds (seals, sea lions, and walruses). Now many classification schemes put pinnipeds in their own mammal group, seperate from the fissiped carnivores.

- **In the Oligocene Epoch** (37–24 mya), fissipeds began to replace creodonts as the dominant carnivores.

- **Fissipeds** were smarter, faster, and deadlier than creodonts, and were the only predators that could catch the new fast-running herbivores.

- **Faster mammals** evolved in the Oligocene Epoch as thick forests changed into open woodlands, with more space to run after, and run from, other creatures.

- **As carnivores evolved**, so they developed bigger brains, more alert senses, sharper claws and teeth, and stronger jaws and limbs.

- **The pinnipeds** are carnivorous mammals that, like whales and dolphins (and reptiles before them), reinvaded the oceans.

····· FASCINATING FACT ·····

Allodesmus was a prehistoric seal. It had flippers, large eyes,
and spiky teeth, which it used to impale slippery fish.

▼ Dinictis *was a fissiped carnivore and member of*
the cat family, which lived in North America about
30 mya. Fissipeds were superbly adapted for
hunting fast-running mammals.

Herbivores

- **The first specialist herbivores** (plant eaters) appeared in the Late Palaeocene Epoch (around 60 mya).

- **They ranged in size** from the equivalent of modern badgers to pigs.

- **These early herbivores** were rooters or browsers—they foraged for food on the floors of their forest homes.

- **It was not until** the very end of the Palaeocene Epoch (58 mya) that the first large herbivores evolved.

- **Large herbivores** emerged before large carnivores. They must have had a peaceful life—for a while!

- *Uintatherium* was one of the large early herbivores. It was the size of a large rhinoceros, with thick limbs to support its heavy body.

- *Uintatherium* had three pairs of bony knobs protruding from its head. Males had very long, strong canine teeth, which they would have used if attacked by creodont carnivores.

- **The growth of grasslands** and the decline of forests in the Miocene Epoch (24–5 mya) speeded up changes to herbivores' bodies.

- **They developed** faster legs to outrun carnivores in open spaces. They also developed better digestive systems to cope with the new, tough grasses.

- **The most important** requirements for a herbivore are complex teeth and digestive systems to break down plant food and release its energy.

▲ Merycoidodon *was a herbivore that lived around 30 mya. It was about the size of a sheep, with a large head and a long body.*

135

Cats

- **Cats** are the most highly developed carnivores. They are the fastest and most intelligent land hunters, with the sharpest claws and teeth.

- **Cats** evolved along two lines. One group was the saber-tooths, which included *Smilodon* (see pages 142–143). This group is extinct today.

- **Saber-tooths** specialized in killing large, heavily-built animals with thick hides, which explains their long canine teeth.

- **The other group** of cats is the felines, which are the ancestors of all modern cats, from lions and cheetahs, to your pet cat.

- **The felines** were faster and more agile than the saber-tooths, who became extinct because their prey became faster and able to outrun them. The felines, however, continued to be successful hunters.

- **One prehistoric feline** was *Dinictis* (see pages p132–133), a puma-sized cat that lived in the Oligocene Epoch (37–24 mya).

- **A later feline** was *Dinofelis,* which lived between 5 and 1.4 mya.

- **The name *Dinofelis*** means "terrible cat." It looked like a modern jaguar, but had stronger front legs that it used to press down on its victims before stabbing them with its teeth.

- ***Dinofelis'*** diet included baboons, antelope, and australopithecines—our human ancestors.

> ...FASCINATING FACT...
> Prehistoric cats' ability to unsheathe and retract their claws provided them with one of their deadliest weapons—and one that cats still have.

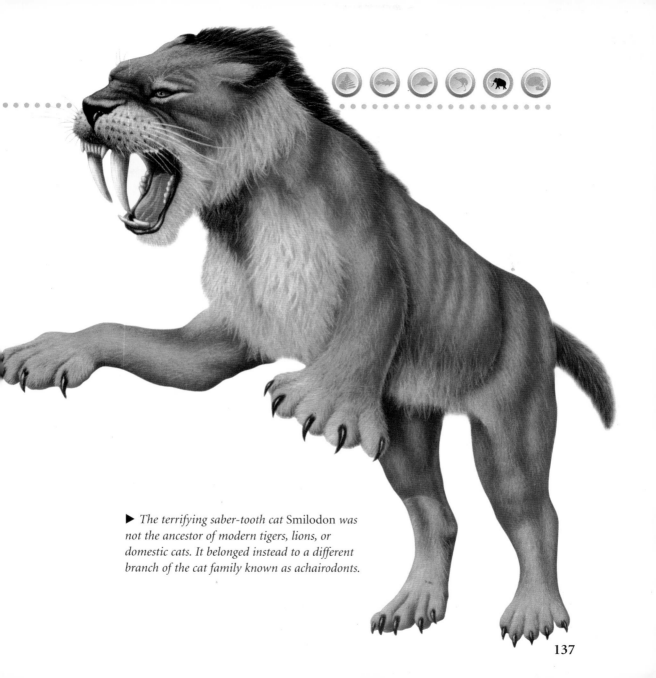

▶ The terrifying saber-tooth cat Smilodon was not the ancestor of modern tigers, lions, or domestic cats. It belonged instead to a different branch of the cat family known as achairodonts.

Dogs

▲ *Part of a pack of* Hesperocyon *dogs, tracking the scent of their prey. Organized hunting in packs is an example of dogs' intelligence.*

- **Early dogs** hunted in a similar way to modern wild dogs—in packs.

- **Dogs** developed long snouts, which gave them a keen sense of smell, and forward-pointing eyes, which gave them good vision.

- **Dogs** also developed a mixture of teeth—sharp canines for stabbing, narrow cheek teeth for slicing and, farther along the jaw, flatter teeth for crushing.

- **These different teeth** meant that dogs could eat a variety of different foods, including plants, which they might have had to eat if meat was in short supply.

- **One of the ancestors** of dogs, as well as bears, was the bear-dog *Amphicyon*. Its name means "in-between dog."

- *Amphicyon* lived between 40 and 9 mya.

- **Trace fossils** of *Amphicyon*'s footprints show that it walked like a bear with its feet flat on the ground.

- *Hesperocyon* was one of the earliest dogs, living between 37 and 29 mya.

- *Hesperocyon* was the size of a small fox. It had long legs and jaws, forward-pointing eyes, and a supple, slender body.

> **...FASCINATING FACT...**
> Hunting in packs allowed *Hesperocyon* to catch large animals
> that it would not have been able to kill on its own.

Andrewsarchus

- *Andrewsarchus* is one of the largest meat-eating land mammals that has ever existed.

- **It lived in East Asia** in the Late Eocene Epoch (around 40 mya).

- **No complete** *Andrewsarchus* skeleton has ever been found—only its skull, which measured 33 in (83 cm) long.

- **Paleontologists** have built up an impression of the rest of the animal's body from knowledge of its skull, and its relation to the earlier, bearlike *Mesonyx*.

- **If their impression** is correct, *Andrewsarchus* was 6 ft (1.8 m) high and 16 ft (5 m) long.

- **It had long**, strong jaws, which it used to eat a variety of foods.

- *Andrewsarchus* was a scavenger and an omnivore—it would eat anything.

- **It belonged** to a group of carnivorous hoofed mammals known as mesonychids.

- **Fossil-hunters** have found most mesonychid remains near prehistoric rivers and coasts, suggesting that this was where they lived and hunted.

▶ *The colossal* Andrewsarchus *lived a bit like a bear. It hunted hoofed mammals but would also have scavenged other predators' leftovers and eaten leaves, berries, and insects.*

...FASCINATING FACT...
Andrewsarchus means "Andrew's flesh-eater." It was named after the naturalist, explorer, and writer Roy Chapman Andrews (1884–1960).

Smilodon

▲ Smilodon *was a fearsome predator. It became extinct because it was not fast enough to catch the quick-running mammals that evolved at the end of the last Ice Age, about 11,000 years ago.*

- **Smilodon** was a terrifying predator that belonged to a group of cats called saber-tooths.

  - **It lived** between 1 million and 11,000 years ago in North and South America.

    - **One of Smilodon's** most distinctive features was its huge, curved canine teeth, which could be up to 10 in (25 cm) long. It could also open its jaws to an angle of about 90 degrees!

      - **The first** saber-tooth was *Megantereon*. It lived about 30 mya.

  - **Smilodon** was only a little larger than a big lion, but was around twice its weight at 441 lb (200 kg).

- **Its "design"** was more like a bear's than a modern cat's—it had very powerful forelegs, a thick neck, and a short spine.

- **Because of its shorter spine** and heavier build, *Smilodon* was not as fast as feline cats (the ancestors of modern cats). It made up for this with its power and its teeth.

- **Smilodon** preyed on large and slow-moving creatures, such as prehistoric bison, mammoths, giant camels, and ground sloths.

- **Smilodon** was truly a top predator, with no real enemies and no direct competitors—until the emergence of modern humans.

> **...FASCINATING FACT...**
> *Smilodon's* large canines were very delicate. They could break when stabbing thick-skinned animals, such as bison.

Paraceratherium

- *Paraceratherium* is the largest land mammal ever to have lived.

- **It was a gentle giant**, which could be as tall as 18 ft (5.5 m) at the shoulder.

- *Paraceratherium* belonged to the group of mammals called perissodactyls—hoofed mammals with an odd number of toes.

- **It was also** an early rhinoceros, but unlike its living relatives, had no horns on its snout.

- **Remains** of this huge beast have been discovered in Europe and Central Asia, where it lived between 30 and 16 mya.

- **Until recently** this beast was known as *Indricotherium*, but it is now more commonly known as *Paraceratherium*.

- *Paraceratherium* had long front legs and a long neck, which it used like a giraffe to reach leaves on the high branches of trees.

- **Males** were larger than females, and had heavier heads with more dome-shaped skulls.

- **In comparison** with the rest of its body, *Paraceratherium*'s skull was quite small.

... FASCINATING FACT ...
Male *Paraceratherium* could be as heavy as 30 tons—
four times the weight of a modern elephant!

▼ Paraceratherium—*also known as*
Indricotherium—*was a giant, hornless,*
long-necked rhinoceros. Although it was
massively heavy, its long legs probably
meant that Paraceratherium *was*
capable of running.

Megatherium

▶ Megatherium, *meaning "great beast" was identified and named by the French naturalist Georges Cuvier (1769–1832).*

146

- *Megatherium* was a giant ground sloth—an extinct type of sloth that lived about 5 mya.

- *Megatherium* stood about 23 ft (7 m) tall. It had huge, extremely strong arms, and massive claws, which it used to pull down branches and even uproot trees.

- **It had short** hind legs and a powerful tail that it used for extra support when it stood up on its rear legs to reach the tallest branches.

- *Megatherium* walked on its knuckles on its forelimbs and on the side of its feet on its hind legs.

- **The sheer size of** *Megatherium* would have put off most predators, but it also had very tough skin—an extra defense.

- **The remains** of ground sloth skin found in caves in South America show that its was made even stronger by tiny lumps of bone.

- *Megatherium* lived in parts of South America, such as present-day Bolivia and Peru.

- **When South America** became joined to North America about 3 mya, *Megatherium* spread northward.

- *Megatherium* is thought to have become extinct 11,000 years ago, but some people in Argentina claim it lived until 400 years ago. If this is so, it is likely that humans killed off the last of these giants.

...FASCINATING FACT...
Megatherium belonged to a group of mammals
called edentates, which lacked front teeth.

Glyptodonts

▲ Glyptodon, *means "grooved tooth." It was named by the English scientist Richard Owen (1804–1892) from fossilized bones that the English naturalist Charles Darwin (1809–1882) brought back with him from South America.*

- **Glyptodonts** were giant armadillos that lived in South America between 5 million and 11,000 years ago.

- **They had domelike shells** and armored tails that ended in a spiked club.

- **Their tail** also served as an extra support when they reared up on their hind legs—either to defend themselves against attackers or to mate.

- **They also had** powerful jaws and huge cheek teeth that could constantly be replaced, unlike most other mammals.

- **These constantly** growing teeth meant they could chew through the toughest plants without wearing down their teeth.

- *Glyptodon* was a 10 ft (3 m) long glyptodont. Like other glyptodonts, it was an edentate—in other words, it did not have front teeth.

- *Doedicurus* was an even bigger glyptodont. It weighed 3,086 lb (1,400 kg) and was 13 ft (4 m) long—the size of a big automobile!

- *Doedicurus* is the most heavily-armored plant eater ever to have lived. A sledgehammer would have made little impression on its massive, bony shell.

- **The body armor** and weaponry of glyptodonts were designed to protect them against predators such as *Thylacosmilus* (see pages 154–155).

... FASCINATING FACT ...
Glyptodonts' armor and tails were similar to those of ankylosaur dinosaurs. This is another example of evolutionary convergence—when separate groups of animals develop similar characteristics.

Bats

- **Icaronycteris** is the earliest-known bat. Its fossil remains are between 55 and 45 million years old.

- **Despite its age,** Icaronycteris looks very similar to a modern bat. It has a bat's typically large ears, which it probably used as a sonar, like modern bats.

- **One difference** from modern bats was that Icaronycteris' tail was not joined to its legs by flaps of skin.

- **Paleontologists** think that there must have been earlier, more primitive-looking bats from which Icaronycteris evolved.

- **The chance of finding** earlier prehistoric bat fossils is very small—like birds, bats have very fragile skeletons that do not fossilize well.

- **Icaronycteris** ate insects. Paleontologists know this because they have found insect remains in the part of the fossil where its stomach would have been.

- **Icaronycteris** fossils have been found in North America.

- **The fossil remains** of another prehistoric bat, *Palaeochiropteryx,* have been found in Europe.

- **Like Icaronycteris**, this bat seems to have been an insectivore (insect eater).

▶ *Like this living bat, prehistoric bats such as* Icaronycteris *probably used sonar to sense nearby objects and hunt for prey. Bats use sonar by making a high-pitched sound and then listening to its echoes.*

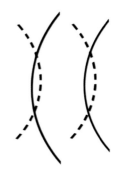

····FASCINATING FACT····
Bats are the only mammals that are known to have
reached Australia after it became isolated from the
rest of the world around 40 mya.

Marsupials

- **Marsupials** are mammals that give birth to their offspring at a very early stage in their development—when they are still tiny.

- **After being born**, the infant crawls through its mother's fur to a pouch called the marsupium, where it stays, feeding on milk, until it is big enough to leave.

- **Paleontologists** think that the first marsupials evolved in North America and then spread to South America and Australia.

- *Alphadon,* meaning "first tooth," was an early marsupial, which emerged around 70 mya. It lived in North and South America.

- *Alphadon* was 12 in (30 cm) long and weighed 11 oz (300 gm). It would have lived in trees, using its feet to climb and fed on insects and small vertebrates.

- **When Australia** became isolated from the rest of the world about 40 mya, its marsupials continued to evolve—unlike the rest of the world, where they fell into decline.

- **Marsupials** continued to exist in South America, which was also isolated from the rest of the world, during much of the Tertiary Period (65–1.6 mya).

- **But when South America** became reconnected with North America, about 3 mya, the arrival of placental mammals from the north led many marsupials to become extinct.

- **Today,** there are only two surviving groups of marsupials in the Americas: the opossums found throughout America and the rat opossums found in South America.

- **Australia** has many living marsupials, from kangaroos to koalas. However, it had a much greater marsupial population in the Tertiary Period—we know this from fossil sites such as Riversleigh in northwest Queensland.

◀ Procoptodon *was a giant kangaroo that stood around 10 ft (3 m) tall. In Australia, plant-eating marsupials such as kangaroos and wallabies occupied the position taken by hoofed mammals in other parts of the world.*

153

Thylacosmilus

- ***Thylacosmilus*** was a carnivorous marsupial. It belonged to a family of South American marsupials called the Borhyaenidae, all of whom had large skulls and teeth.

- **It lived and hunted** on the grassy plains of South America in the Pliocene Epoch (5–1.6 mya).

- ***Thylacosmilus*** **was about the size** of a modern jaguar, growing up to 4 ft (1.2 m) long and weighing about 253.5 lb (115 kg).

▲ While Thylacosmilus *had much in common with saber-tooth cats, it had some differences too. Unlike true cats, it was a marsupial, its saber-teeth never stopped growing and it could not retract its claws.*

- **There are some** amazing similarities between *Thylacosmilus* and the saber-tooth cats, such as *Smilodon*.

- **Like *Smilodon***, *Thylacosmilus* had very long, upper canine teeth, which it used to stab its prey.

- **Also like *Smilodon***, *Thylacosmilus* had very powerful shoulder and neck muscles, which meant it could press its huge canines down with great force.

- **This is remarkable** because the saber-tooths were placental mammals that evolved in North America and *Thylacosmilus* was a marsupial that evolved in South America at a time when the two continents were not connected.

- **It is another example** of evolutionary convergence—when separate groups of animals develop similar characteristics.

- **Unlike the saber-toothed cats,** however, *Thylacosmilus'* teeth continued to grow throughout its life.

- ***Thylacosmilus*** became extinct after the land bridge between North and South America was re-established. It could not compete with the more powerful carnivores that arrived from the north.

155

Elephant evolution

· ·

- **Elephants** and their ancestors belong to an order of animals called Proboscidea, meaning "long-snoute." Another word for elephants is proboscideans.

- **The ancestors** of elephants appeared around 40 mya. They were trunkless and looked a bit like large pigs.

- *Moeritherium* is the earliest known of these elephant ancestors. Its name comes from Lake Moeris in Egypt, where fossil-hunters first discovered its remains.

- **It was 10 ft (3 m) long** and weighed 441 lb (200 kg), and probably spent much of its life wallowing in rivers or shallow lakes, like a hippopotamus.

- **The next step** in the development of elephants was taken by *Phiomia,* which lived about 36 mya.

- *Phiomia* had a well-formed trunk as well as two pairs of tusks—a pair on its upper jaw, projecting out and then down, and a pair on its lower jaw.

- *Phiomia* is the first-known of a group of elephants called mastodonts. Its shoulder height could be up to 8 ft (2.4 m), and it lived in swampy areas.

- **One group** of elephants that descended from *Phiomia* were the deinotheres, which had one pair of enormous downward curving tusks in the lower jaw.

- **The other groups** that evolved from the mastodonts were the true elephants (which resemble living elephants) and the mammoths. These animals appeared in the Pliocene Epoch (5–1.6 mya).

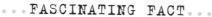

··· FASCINATING FACT ···
Mammoths were giant elephants. The first
mammoth was possibly *Stegodon*, which had very
long tusks and lived in Asia and Africa.

▼ *The hippopotamus-like* Moeritherium. *The American paleontologist Henry Fairfield Osborn (1857–1935) described it as "a missing link" between elephants and other mammals.*

Platybelodon

- *Platybelodon* was an early—but not the first—member of a group of prehistoric elephants called mastodonts.
- **It lived about** 25 mya in the cold northern regions of Europe, Asia, and North America.
- *Platybelodon's* lower jaw ended in two very wide, flat tusks—like a pair of spades.
- *Platybelodon* is known as "shovel-tusker," because paleontologists think it used its tusks as a shovel to scoop up plants.
- **It also** had flat cheek teeth, sharp front teeth, and a very wide trunk.
- **This mastodont** had a pair of tusks on its upper jaw, too. They slotted into an indentation near the top of its lower tusks when *Platybelodon* closed its mouth.
- *Platybelodon* **was 20 ft (6 m) long** and weighed between 4 and 5 tons.
- **The time period** in which *Platybelodon* lived was quite short compared to other animals, and other species of elephant in particular.
- **This is probably** because *Platybelodon* was a very specialized feeder and was vulnerable to any climate change that would affect the sort of plants it ate.

> ...FASCINATING FACT...
> The first elephants lived in Africa but— as discoveries of
> *Platybelodon* fossils have shown—they migrated to Europe,
> Asia, and then North America.

▲ *Scientists used to think that* Platybelodon *fed on soft water plants. Recent research on its fossilized tusks suggests that it ate much tougher material, such as the branches of trees.*

159

Wooly mammoth

▶ *In 1994, scientists discovered DNA, or genetic material, in the fossil remains of a wooly mammoth. They found that it was nearly identical to the DNA of living elephants.*

- **Wooly mammoths** (scientific name *Mammuthus primigenius*) lived between 120,000 and 6,000 years ago.

- **They lived** on the steppes of Russia and Asia and the plains of North America during the ice ages of the Quaternary Period (1.6 mya to the present).

  - **To survive** these cold places, wooly mammoths were designed for warmth and insulation.

    - **Their wooly coats** were made up of two layers of hair—an outside layer of long, coarse hairs, and a second layer of densely packed bristles.

    - **They also had** very tough skins—up to 1 in (2.5 cm) thick—beneath which was a deep layer of fat.

    - **Male wooly mammoths** could grow up to 11.5 ft (3.5 m) long and 9.5 ft (2.9 m) high at the shoulder, and weigh up to 2.75 tons.

- **They had** long tusks that curved forward, up, and then back. They used their tusks to defend themselves against attackers and, probably, to clear snow and ice to reach low-lying plants.

- **Some cave paintings** by Cro-Magnon humans (see page 200) clearly depict wooly mammoths.

- **Many excellently preserved** wooly mammoth remains have been discovered in the permanently frozen ground of Siberia.

> . . . **FASCINATING FACT** . . .
> People often think the wooly mammoth had red hair, but in fact this color was a chemical reaction that happened after the animal died.

Columbian mammoth

- **The Columbian mammoth** (scientific name *Mammuthus columbi*) was an even bigger species than the wooly mammoth.

- **Its coat** was not as thick as the wooly mammoth's, and it lived in warmer regions, including North America and Mexico.

- **The Columbian mammoth** grew up to 14 ft (4.2 m) high at the shoulder, and weighed over 10 tons—the equivalent of 130 adult humans!

- **It needed to eat** more than 772 lb (350 kg) of plant food every day to keep itself going, and to drink about 42 gal (160 l) of water.

- **It used** its powerful trunk for feeding, as well as for moving and breaking things.

- **This trunk** was like an extra arm. It had two finger-like projections at the end, which could grab hold of objects.

- **Its tusks** could grow up to 16 ft (5 m) long. It used these for fighting rival mammoths and defending themselves against predators.

- **Some scientists** think that the Columbian mammoth was actually the same species as the imperial mammoth (scientific name *Mammuthus imperator*). The imperial mammoth was one of the largest mammoths ever to have lived, estimated by some to have stood 16 ft (4.8 m) high at the shoulder.

- **Both the Columbian** and the imperial mammoths lacked thick coats and lived in relatively warm climates.

- **The imperial mammoth's** tusks, however, were much more twisted than those of the Columbian mammoth.

▲ *Early humans in North America hunted the Columbian mammoth, a fact known from finds of tools and building materials made out of the mammoth's bone.*

The first horses

▼ Hyracotherium *is the earliest known horse. Over time, horses became the best-adapted of all hoofed animals for life on the open plains.*

- **Horses** have one of the best fossil records of any animal, so paleontologists have been able to trace their evolution from the earliest horselike mammals to the modern horse.

- *Hyracotherium* is the first-known horse. It lived in forests in North America and Europe in the Late Palaeocene and Early Eocene Epochs (60–50 mya).

- **Another name** for *Hyracotherium* is *Eohippus,* which means "dawn horse."

- *Hyracotherium* was the size of a fox. It had a short neck, a long tail and slender limbs. It also had three toes on its hind feet and four toes on its front feet.

- *Mesohippus* was one of the next horses to evolve after *Hyracotherium,* between 40 and 25 mya. Its name means "middle horse."

- *Mesohippus* had longer legs than *Hyracotherium* and would have been a faster runner.

- **It would also** have been better at chewing food, because its teeth had a larger surface area.

- **An improved** chewing ability was important for horses and other plant-eaters as forests gave way to grasslands, and more abundant but tougher plants.

- *Mesohippus* had also evolved three toes on its front feet to match the three on its hind feet.

- **As horses** evolved, they migrated from North America and Europe to Asia, Africa, and South America.

Later horses

- *Merychippus,* which lived between 11 and 5 mya, represented a leap forward from earlier horses, such as *Mesohippus*. It was the size of a pony.

- **It was the first horse** to eat only grass, and—to help it reach the grass—had a longer neck and muzzle (snout) than earlier horses.

- *Merychippus'* middle toe had also evolved into a hoof, although this hoof did not have a pad on the bottom, unlike modern horses.

- **The legs** of *Merychippus* were designed for outrunning carnivores. Its upper leg bones were shorter than previous horses, the lower leg bones were longer.

- **Shorter upper leg bones** meant that the horse's main leg-moving muscles could be packed in at the top of the leg—which translates into a faster-running animal.

- *Hipparion,* which means "better horse," was a further advance on *Merychippus*. It had thinner legs and more horse-like hooves.

- *Hipparion* lived between 15 and 2 mya.

- *Pliohippus* was an even more advanced horse. The side toes that *Hipparion* still had, had vanished on *Pliohippus,* making it the first one-toed horse.

- *Pliohippus'* teeth were similar to those of modern horses—they were long and had an uneven surface for grinding up grass.

- *Equus*, the modern horse and the latest stage in the evolution of the animal, first appeared around 2 mya.

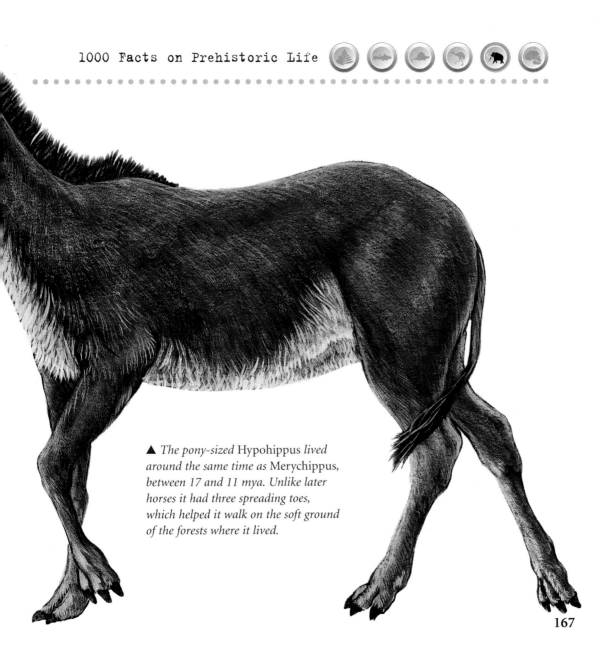

▲ *The pony-sized* Hypohippus *lived around the same time as* Merychippus, *between 17 and 11 mya. Unlike later horses it had three spreading toes, which helped it walk on the soft ground of the forests where it lived.*

The first whales

- **The very first whales** looked nothing like the enormous creatures that swim in our oceans today.

- *Ambulocetus*, one of the first members of the whale family, looked more like a giant otter. It lived about 50 mya.

- *Ambulocetus* means "walking whale," and it spent more time on land than in water.

- **It would**, however, have been a good swimmer. Fossil remains show that *Ambulocetus* had webbed feet and hands.

- **An even earlier** whale ancestor than *Ambulocetus* was *Pakicetus*, which lived about 52 mya.

- *Pakicetus* is named after the country Pakistan, where a fossil of its skull was found in 1979.

- *Pakicetus* was around 6 ft (1.8 m) long. *Ambulocetus*, at 10 ft (3 m), was bigger.

▲ Pakicetus *could run fast and swim well.*
It probably lived alongside rivers and streams
and hunted animals both in and out of the water.

- **Paleontologists** think that whales evolved from carnivorous hoofed mammals called mesonychids.

- **Around 40 mya**, the first true whales, which swam only, evolved from their half-walking, half-swimming ancestors.

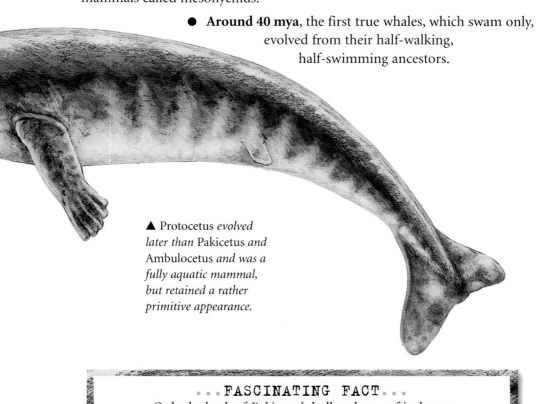

▲ Protocetus *evolved later than* Pakicetus *and* Ambulocetus *and was a fully aquatic mammal, but retained a rather primitive appearance.*

...FASCINATING FACT...
Only the back of *Pakicetus'* skull and part of its lower jaw have been found. From this, however, paleontologists can tell it was not able to dive very deeply.

Later whales

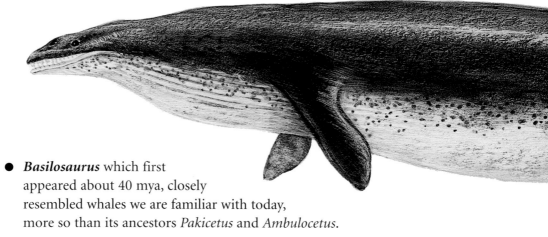

- **Basilosaurus** which first appeared about 40 mya, closely resembled whales we are familiar with today, more so than its ancestors *Pakicetus* and *Ambulocetus*.

- **It was also enormous!** It measured between 66–82 ft (20–25 m) long—the same as three elephants standing in a row.

- **It had** a variety of teeth in its mouth—sharp teeth at the front for stabbing, and saw-edged teeth at the back for chewing.

- **Basilosaurus** ate large fish, squid, and other marine mammals.

- **There were some** big differences between *Basilosaurus* and modern whales. For a start, it had a slimmer body.

> **...FASCINATING FACT...**
> *Cetotherium* was a prehistoric baleen whale that first appeared 15 mya. Instead of teeth, these whales had hard plates in their mouths called baleen that filtered plankton and small fish.

▼ *The prehistoric whale* Basilosaurus, *which means "king of the lizards," was so named because the first person to examine its remains thought it was a gigantic plesiosaur—a prehistoric marine reptile.*

- **It also lacked** a blowhole, a nostril on the top of modern whales' heads that they breathe out of when they come to the surface. Instead, *Basilosaurus* had nostrils on its snout.

- *Prosqualodon* did have a blowhole and was a more advanced whale than *Basilosaurus*. It lived between 30 and 20 mya.

- **It may have been** the ancestor of toothed whales, a group that includes sperm whales, killer whales, beaked whales, and dolphins.

- *Prosqualodon* looked similar to a dolphin. It had a long, streamlined body and a long, narrow snout, which was full of pointed teeth.

171

Megaloceros

▲ *Scientists used to believe that, because* Megaloceros' *antlers were so big, they could only have been used for display purposes—to scare off rivals. In the 1980s however, research proved that these antlers were used for fighting.*

- *Megaloceros* is one of the largest species of deer ever to have lived. Adult males were 7.2 ft (2.2 m) long, 7 ft (2 m) tall at the shoulders and weighed 1,543 lb (700 kg).

- **This deer** lived between 400,000 and 9,000 years ago.

- *Megaloceros* is known as the Irish elk because a large number of fossils of the species have been discovered in Ireland, particularly in peat bogs.

- But *Megaloceros* lived all over Europe, the Middle East, China, and North America, too.

- *Megaloceros* had a much broader, flatter snout than modern deer, which suggests that it was a less fussy eater and just hoovered up plant food in enormous quantities.

- **Like modern deer,** *Megaloceros* males shed their antlers and grew another pair every year. For antlers as big as *Megaloceros*', this required a huge intake of nutrients and minerals.

- **About 10,000 years ago,** falling temperatures led the dwarf willow bush—a major source of the nutrients *Megaloceros* needed to grow its antlers—to decline.

- **This food shortage** is one theory as to why *Megaloceros* became extinct.

- **Another theory** is that early humans, who greatly prized *Megaloceros*' antlers, hunted it to extinction.

> ...**FASCINATING FACT**...
> Megaloceros was a fast runner—it could move at around
> 50 mph (80 km/h.) It used this turn of speed to escape
> from predators such as wolves.

Early primates

- **The primates** are a group of mammals that include lemurs, monkeys, apes, and humans.

- **Primates** have a much greater range of movement in their arms, legs, fingers, and toes than other mammals.

- **They also have** a more acute sense of touch because their fingers and toes end in flat nails, not curved claws—so the skin on the other side evolved into a sensitive pad.

- **The ancestors** of primates were small insectivorous (insect-eating) mammals that looked like shrews.

- **The first known primate** was *Plesiadapis,* which lived about 60 mya in Europe and North America. It was a squirrel-like tree climber.

- **More advanced primates** developed about 10 million years later. They looked a bit like modern lemurs.

- *Notharctus* was one of these lemur-like primates. It ate leaves and fruit, was about 16 in (40 cm) long, and had a grasping thumb that would have gripped well to branches.

- **Other more advanced**, but still early, primates includes *Smilodectes* and *Tetonius*. They had larger brains and eyes, longer tails, and smaller snouts than *Plesiadapis*.

- **These animals** were the ancestors of tarsiers, lemurs, and lorises, but not the higher primates—the monkeys, apes, and humans. Paleontologists believe that role belongs to the omomyid primates.

- **One early monkey** was *Mesopithecus,* which lived 8 mya in Greece and Turkey. It was similar to modern monkeys in many ways, but had a longer tail.

174

▲ *The early primate* Plesiadapis *had a long tail and claws on its fingers and toes— unlike later monkeys and apes, which had nails.*

175

Apes

▶ *The early ape* Dryopithecus *stood about 3 ft (1 m) tall. It had the largest brain for its size of any mammal and flourished in open grassland regions in Africa, Asia, and Europe.*

● **Apes** are primates that have more complex brains than monkeys and no tails. Hominids (early humans) evolved from apes.

● *Aegyptopithecus* was one of the ancestors of apes. It lived in Egypt in the Oligocene Epoch (37–24 mya). It was small and had a short tail.

- ***Proconsul,*** which lived between 23 and 14 mya, was an early ape. Its body size varied from that of a small monkey to that of a female gorilla, and had a larger brain than *Aegyptopithecus*.

- ***Proconsul*** was a fruit eater. Paleontologists think that it walked on four limbs with part of its weight supported by the knuckles of its hands, like modern chimpanzees and gorillas.

- **Two lines of apes** developed after *Proconsul*. From one line came gibbons and orangutans, from the other chimpanzees, gorillas, and humans.

- ***Dryopithecus*** was a chimplike ape that evolved after *Proconsul* and lived in the Miocene Epoch (24–5 mya). It may have stood on two legs but climbed using all four.

- ***Ramapithecus*** was an ape that lived in the Middle and Late Miocene Epoch. It is now thought to be part of the chain of evolution of Asian apes and is possibly an ancestor of the orangutan.

- **Australopithecines** were a further step in the evolution from apes to humans. Australopithecines (meaning "southern apes") walked on two legs.

- **The biggest-ever ape** was *Gigantopithecus,* which lived in China until around 1 mya. It may have been up to 8 ft (2.5 m) tall and weighed 661 lb (300 kg).

. . . FASCINATING FACT . . .
Proconsul was named in 1927 after Consul, a performing chimpanzee that appeared on stage smoking a pipe and riding a bicycle.

Walking upright

- **Hominidae** is the "human family" of ourselves and our ancestors and prehistoric relatives. Hominids (humans) differed from apes by walking on two legs, not four.

- **Fossils** of hominids' backbones, neck, foot, and leg bones demonstrate their evolution from apes that walked on all fours.

- **Hominids'** spines developed an S-shaped curve so that the hips supported the weight of the upper body. Apes' spines have just one curve.

- **The heads of the hominids** evolved to sit on the top of the spine, while apes' heads sit at the front of the spine.

- **Hominids'** feet became long and flat to support the rest of the body when they walked. Apes' feet have curved toes to grasp onto branches for climbing.

- **The leg bones of hominids** became longer and straighter than those of apes, so they could walk greater distances more effortlessly.

- **Walking on two legs** helped hominids to cover greater distances in the open grasslands of Africa where they lived.

- **It also allowed them** to see above tall grasses, an advantage when it came to looking for food or keeping a lookout for danger.

- **Upright walking** also freed their arms to do other things, such as carrying babies or food.

> ...**FASCINATING FACT**...
> The first fossilized footprints of an upright walker
> were discovered in 1978. They belong to
> *Australopithecus afarensis*, which lived 3.8 mya.

Homo habilis

Homo erectus

Homo neanderthalensis

Homo sapiens

▲ *Experts agree that the adoption of upright walking was one of the most important developments in the history of hominids. It freed the arms and hands to carry objects, making the body look bigger to potential predators and keeping it cool in the hot Sun.*

Offspring

- **Human parents** look after their children for a longer period than any other animal.

- **A close bond** between parents and children is also a feature of modern primates—and would have been so for prehistoric primates, too.

- **This is because humans** and primates have small numbers of infants compared to many other animals, and females are pregnant for longer.

- **There is also** a longer period of upbringing for humans and primates than for other animals—during which time offspring learn survival and social skills.

- **As with apes**, the pelvises of early hominids were quite wide, which meant that their offspring were quite large when they were born.

- **Like modern humans**, later hominids—from *Homo ergaster* on— had smaller pelvises, which meant that their babies were smaller and less developed when born.

- **Smaller** and less developed babies require more nurture and protection— as a result, childcare became an even bigger concern for hominids.

- **This change** led to other ones. Hominid groups increased in size, so that the responsibility for childcare could be spread around.

- **There was also** more cooperation between males and females and they began to pair-up in partnerships.

- **Such partnerships** were mutually beneficial—the female could look after the offspring while the male provided food. In turn, the male could be certain that the offspring was his own.

▲ *A female orangutan with its infant. Primates have closer relationships with their young than other animals, but this is particularly true for humans. Unlike monkeys and apes, human babies cannot move around independently soon after birth, and are very dependant on their mothers.*

181

Early hominids

▲ Ardipithecus ramidus. *Scientists gave it its name from the Afar language of Ethiopia—"ardi" means "ground" while "ramid" means "root"—words that express its position at the base of human history.*

- **One of the earliest-known** hominids (early humans) is *Ardipithecus ramidus,* which lived about 4.5 mya.

- **It would have looked** similar to a chimpanzee in many ways, except for one major difference, *Ardipithecus ramidus* walked on two legs.

- **It lived** in woods and forests, sleeping in trees at night, but foraging on the ground for roots during the day.

- **A full-grown** *Ardipithecus ramidus* male was about 4.3 ft (1.3 m) tall and weighed about 60 lb (27 kg).

- **Archaeologists** discovered the teeth, skull and arm bone fossils of *Ardipithecus ramidus* in Ethiopia in 1994.

- **In 2001,** archeologists in Ethiopia found the remains of an even older hominid, *Ardipithecus ramidus kadabba,* which lived between 5.6 and 5.8 mya.

- **The fossils** of *Ardipithecus ramidus kadabba* are similar to those of *Ardipithecus ramidus,* so it is possible that both are very closely related.

- **Some scientists argue,** however, that *Ardipithecus ramidus kadabba* is closer to an ape than a hominid.

- *Australopithecus anamensis* is a later hominid than *Ardipithecus ramidus.* Its fossils date to between 4.2 and 3.9 million years old.

- **A fossil** of one of *Australopithecus anamensis'* knee-joints shows that it shifted its weight from one leg to the other when it moved—a sure sign that it walked on two legs.

Sahelanthropus tchadensis

- **In 2002**, a team of French archeologists announced the discovery of a new species called *Sahelanthropus tchadensis,* which may be a missing link between apes and early hominids.

- **The archeologists** discovered a near-complete fossil skull of *Sahelanthropus tchadensis*, which has been dated to between 7 and 6 million years old.

- **They also** found the fossils of two pieces of jawbone and three teeth.

- **The French team** found the skull not in East Africa, like all the other early hominids, but in Chad, in central Africa.

- **Finding the skull** in Chad indicates that early hominids ranged well beyond East Africa, where scientists previously believed all early hominids lived.

- **The archeologists** who discovered the skull nicknamed it Toumaï, meaning "hope of life" in Goran, an African language.

- **Despite its great age,** *Sahelanthropus tchadensis'* skull suggests that it had a surprisingly human face, which protruded less than apes.

- *Sahelanthropus tchadensis* also had heavy ridges for its eyebrows. Some archeologists believe that, because of this, it was closer to an ape than a hominid, since female apes have similar heavy ridges.

- **Like later hominids**, *Sahelanthropus tchadensis* had small canine teeth and did not grind its teeth in the same way as apes.

- *Sahelanthropus tchadensis* lived alongside a diverse range of animals. Other fossil finds in the same region include more than 700 types of fish, crocodiles, and rodents.

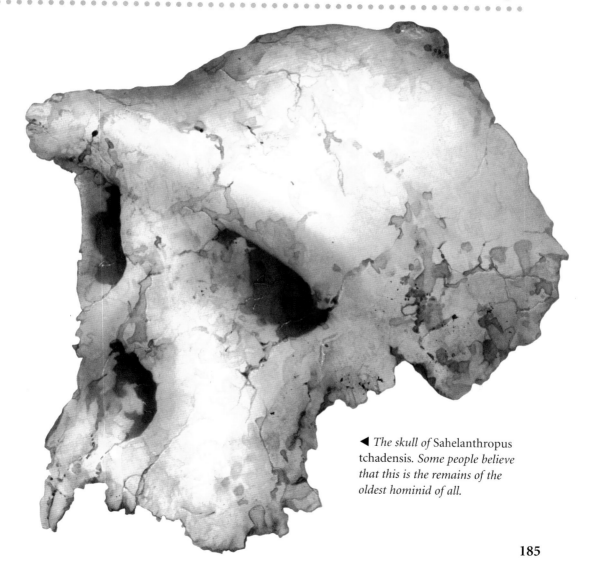

◀ *The skull of* Sahelanthropus tchadensis. *Some people believe that this is the remains of the oldest hominid of all.*

Australopithecus afarensis

- *Australopithecus afarensis* was an early hominid that lived 3.5 mya.

- **Its brain** was the size of a modern chimpanzee's, and it had the short legs and long arms of modern apes.

- *Australopithecus afarensis* was small—between 35–47 in (90–120 cm) from head to toe.

- **Like other** australopithecines, it walked on two legs. This was the most efficient way for it to move over grassland in search of food.

- **It had a wider pelvis** and shorter legs than modern humans. This may have made it a more efficient walker than modern humans.

- *Australopithecus afarensis* ate seeds, fruits, nuts, and occasionally meat.

- **These hominids** had a brief childhood, reaching adulthood at the age of 11 years old. They lived for a maximum of 50 years.

- **Fossil footprints** of *Australopithecus afarensis* show that their feet were similar to ours, although their big toes may have been more apelike.

- **The first fossils** of *Australopithecus afarensis* to be discovered belonged to a female. They were found by American anthropologists Donald Johanson and Tom Gray in 1974, at Hadar in Ethiopia.

. . . FASCINATING FACT . . .
Johanson and Gray named the female "Lucy" after the Beatles' song "Lucy in the Sky with Diamonds," which they listened to on the day of their discovery.

▲ Australopithecus afarensis *spent its days on the ground, foraging for food, but at night may have slept in trees.*

Homo habilis

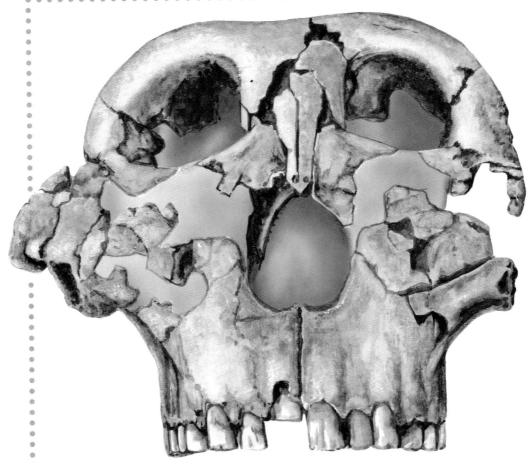

▲ *The first* Homo habilis *skull found by Louis and Mary Leakey in Tanzania. Homo habilis had a bigger brain than any previous hominid.*

- *Homo habilis* is one of the earliest-known members of the genus *Homo*, to which we also belong.

- *Homo habilis* lived between 2.4 and 1.6 mya.

- **The archeologists** Louis and Mary Leakey first discovered its remains at Olduvai Gorge in Tanzania, in 1961.

- **Fossils** of *Homo habilis'* skulls have since been found around Lake Turkana in Kenya, one of the richest sites for hominid fossils in the world.

- **The skulls** show that *Homo habilis* had a flat face with prominent cheekbones, similar to australopithecines, which it would have lived alongside.

- *Homo habilis* was much more apelike than its successor, *Homo ergaster*. It had fur and lacked any form of language.

- **It did have** a bigger brain than any australopithecine. It also had more flexible hands and straighter, more sensitive fingers.

- *Homo habilis* means "handy man"—it could use its hands to gather fruit and crack nuts. It also created the first stone tools.

- **A fully grown** *Homo habilis* male was around 5 ft (1.5 m) tall and weighed about 110 lb (50 kg).

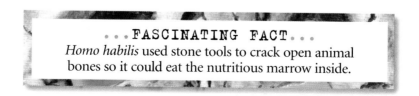

...FASCINATING FACT...
Homo habilis used stone tools to crack open animal bones so it could eat the nutritious marrow inside.

Homo ergaster

- *Homo ergaster* was the first "human-looking" early human. It first appeared about 1.9 mya.

- **Adult males** grew to approximately 70 in (180 cm) tall, with long, slender limbs and a straight spine.

- *Homo ergaster* was the first smooth-skinned hominid, unlike its hairy ancestors. Like us it cooled down by sweating, not panting, which is how earlier hominids cooled themselves.

- **It was also** the first hominid to have a protruding nose—previous hominids merely had nostrils on the surface of their face.

- *Homo ergaster* was generally a scavenger, although it would hunt and kill older or weaker animals.

- **Scientists** know that it ate a lot of meat because one of the skeletons that have been found shows evidence of a bone disease caused by eating too many animal livers.

- **Fossil remains** of *Homo ergaster* were first discovered in 1975. But the most complete skeleton was found in 1984.

- **The skeleton** belonged to a teenage boy named Nariokotome Boy after the site in Lake Turkana, Kenya, where it was found.

- **The structure** of Nariokotome Boy's bones suggest that he was much stronger than modern humans.

- *Homo ergaster* was the first hominid to travel beyond Africa. One place where its remains have been found is Dmanisi, in the Republic of Georgia, near Russia.

► Homo ergaster *was different from any previous hominid. It was taller, with a face that was more lightly built and had smaller cheek teeth.*

Homo erectus

- *Homo erectus* may be a descendant of *Homo ergaster*.

- **It was** virtually identical to its immediate ancestor, except that it had thicker bones in its skull and a more protruding eyebrow ridge.

- *Homo erectus* and *Homo ergaster* lived alongside each other for 2 million years.

- **While *Homo ergaster*** became extinct about 600,000 years ago, *Homo erectus* survived until less than 50,000 years ago.

- **Like its ancestor,** *Homo erectus* spread beyond Africa and settled in Europe and Asia.

- **In the late 19th century,** Eugène Dubois discovered *Homo erectus* fossils on the Indonesian island of Java. He was a famous Dutch paleoanthropologist (someone who studies hominid fossils).

- **In the 1930s,** archeologists discovered more than 40 *Homo erectus* skeletons in China.

- **The archeologists** also found evidence that *Homo erectus* used fire and practiced cannibalism!

- **For a long time**, people called the human to which the Chinese fossils belonged "Peking Man." It was much later that paleoanthropologists realized it was, in fact, *Homo erectus*.

> ...**FASCINATING FACT**...
> The "Peking Man" fossils disappeared at the beginning of World War II and have never been found. They were confiscated by Japanese troops just when they were about to be shipped to the U.S.A.

▲ *Stone hearths in caves that were used by* Homo erectus *prove that it had mastered fire.*
Fire provided warmth, light, protection, and the means to cook food.

Homo heidelbergensis

▲ Homo heidelbergensis *was a superb hunter who used stones, wooden spears, and even stone blades to capture food.*

● ***Homo heidelbergensis*** lived between 600,000 and 250,000 years ago in Africa and Europe.

● **It was the first** hominid to settle in the cold territories of northern Europe.

- **Homo heidelbergensis** had a body much like ours, but its head was rather different, with a heavier jaw, a minimal chin, a flat nose, and thick eyebrow ridges.

- **The teeth** of *Homo heidelbergensis* were 50 percent longer than ours.

- **They also** had a much thicker covering of enamel, which suggests that this species ate the tough parts of animals' flesh and maybe used its teeth for gripping objects.

- **Toward the end** of its existence, *Homo heidelbergensis* would have lived alongside Neanderthals in the same territories.

- *Homo heidelbergensis* is named after the city of Heidelberg in Germany. It was near there that one of the hominid's jawbones was found in 1907.

- **The greatest find** of *Homo heidelbergensis'* fossils was made in a cave system in the Atapuerca hills of northern Spain, in 1976. Archeologists discovered the remains of 32 individuals.

- **In the mid 1990s,** archeologists unearthed *Homo heidelbergensis* bones, tools, and animal carcasses in Boxgrove, England. The carcasses had been expertly stripped of all their meat.

> ...FASCINATING FACT...
> Unlike the Neanderthals that came later, there is no
> evidence that *Homo heidelbergensis* buried its dead.

Homo neanderthalensis

- **Homo neanderthalensis**—or Neanderthals—lived between 230,000 and 28,000 years ago across Europe, Russia, and parts of the Middle East.

▶ *A Neanderthal campsite. The remains of a tent peg at one site suggests that Neanderthals were capable of making tentlike structures, although they also lived in cave mouths and rock shelters.*

- **Homo neanderthalensis means** "man from the Neander Valley," which is the site in Germany where the first of its fossil remains were found in 1865.

- **Neanderthals** are our extinct cousins rather than our direct ancestors— they are from a different branch of the human family.

- **They were** about 30 percent heavier than modern humans. Their bodies were more sturdy and they had shorter legs.

- **Neanderthals'** shorter, stockier bodies were better suited than modern humans to life in Europe and Russia during the ice ages of the Pleistocene Epoch (1.6 million to 10,000 years ago).

- **Their faces** were also different, with sloping foreheads and heavy brow ridges.

- **They buried** their dead, cooked meat, and made various tools and weapons.

- **Neanderthals** made the first ever spears tipped with stone blades.

- **For about 10,000 years** Neanderthals lived alongside modern humans in Europe, before becoming extinct.

> ....**FASCINATING FACT**...
> Many people think that Neanderthals were slow and stupid, but in fact
> their brains were at least as big as modern human's.

Homo floresiensis

- **In 2004**, Australian paleoanthropologists discovered an entirely new species of human, *Homo floresiensis,* which lived on the Indonesian island of Flores between 95,000 and 13,000 years ago.

- **In total**, paleoanthropologists have unearthed the remains of seven individuals.

- **The most complete**, although still partial, skeleton, is that of a female. Study of one of its leg bones shows that it was an upright walker.

- **The discovery** changes scientists' understanding of human evolution—beforehand, it was assumed that *Homo sapiens* had been the sole remaining human species since the disappearance of Neanderthal humans about 30,000 years ago.

- **Paleoanthropologists** nicknamed *Homo floresiensis* "hobbit man" because of its tiny size. It was about 3 ft (1 m) tall, and had a brain the size of a chimpanzee's.

- **Its small brain size** does not seem to have reflected its intelligence however—*Homo floresiensis* was a skilled toolmaker, producing finely crafted stone tools.

- **Flores**, off the coast of mainland Asia, has been an island for over a million years. Being small represents an adaptation to living on an isolated island, where resources were limited.

- *Homo floresiensis'* small size challenges the accepted belief that humans modify their surroundings to suit themselves. Some people believe that, on the contrary, this human species evolved into a smaller creature to cope with its island habitat.

- **Local inhabitants** of Flores have long told stories of little hairy people called *ebu gogo*, meaning "grandmother who eats anything," which used to live on the island.

- *Homo floresiensis* was a hunter. One of the animals it preyed on was the pygmy elephant. Both *Homo floresiensis,* and the pygmy elephants seem to have become extinct after a volcanic eruption about 12,000 years ago.

▲ *Two* Homo floresiensis *hunters prepare to attack a pygmy elephant. The discovery of this new species of human challenges our ideas of human evolution.*

Homo sapiens

- *Homo sapiens*—meaning "wise man"—first appeared in Africa around 150,000 years ago. This is the species to which human beings belong.

- **The first** *Homo sapiens* outside Africa appeared in Israel, 90,000 years ago.

- **By 40,000 years ago**, *Homo sapiens* had spread to many parts of the world, including Europe and Borneo.

- **We call the humans** that settled in Europe Cro-Magnons. They dressed in furs and hunted with spears and nets.

- **Cro-Magnons** had a basic language and culture, which included painting images on cave walls.

- **They were** very similar to modern humans, but with marginally bigger jaws and noses and more rounded braincases (the part of the skull that encloses the brain).

- *Homo sapiens* probably arrived in North America about 30,000 years ago.

- **They would have** crossed the Bering land bridge—formed by shrunken sea levels during the then ice age—from present-day Siberia to present-day Alaska.

- **The earliest known** human culture in North America is that of the Clovis people, which is thought to be around 11,500 years old.

> ...**FASCINATING FACT**...
> Humans living today have evolved only slightly from the earliest *Homo sapiens*. Our full scientific name is *Homo sapiens sapiens*, which means "the wise wise man."

▲ *Cave painting, cooking, and complicated tool-making are all features of early* Homo sapiens. Homo sapiens *also look different from other human species, having a higher forehead and a more prominent chin.*

Brains and intelligence

- **Primates**, from which hominids descended, had bigger brains in relation to their body size than other mammals.

- **Primates developed** larger brains—and more intelligence—because living in and moving between trees required a high degree of balance, coordination and the skilful use of hands and feet.

- **Once hominids' brains** started getting bigger, their skulls began to change. Bigger brains led to the development of foreheads.

- *Homo habilis'* **brain** was 50 percent bigger than its australopithecine predecessors. It had a brain capacity of 25 fl oz (750 ml).

- **The structure** of its brain was different to that of earlier hominids. It had bigger frontal lobes—the parts of the brain associated with problem-solving.

- *Homo habilis* put its greater intelligence to use in the quest to find meat, which it scavenged from other animals' kills to supplement its diet.

- **Eating more meat** allowed hominids' brains to get even bigger. Breaking down plant food uses up a huge amount of energy, so the fewer plants hominids ate, the more energy was available for their brains.

- *Homo ergaster* had an even bigger brain, with a capacity of around 34 fl oz (1,000 ml). It could use this intelligence to read tracks left by animals—a major development in hunting.

- **The brain** of *Homo erectus* became larger during its existence. About 1 mya its brain capacity was 34 fl oz (1000 ml); 500,000 years later it was 44 fl oz (1300 ml).

- **Our brain capacity** is 1750 ml.

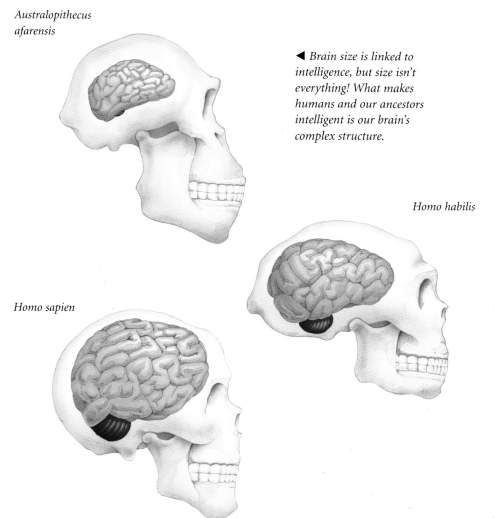

Australopithecus afarensis

◀ *Brain size is linked to intelligence, but size isn't everything! What makes humans and our ancestors intelligent is our brain's complex structure.*

Homo habilis

Homo sapien

Tools

▶ Homo habilis *produced flakes of stone, such as this one, by striking one stone against another, called a hammerstone.*

Stone tool

- **The greatest number** of *Homo habilis* tools has been found in the Olduvai Gorge in Tanzania. They include rocks that were used as hammers, flakers, choppers, and scrapers.

- *Homo habilis* used these tools to cut meat and, especially, to scrape open animal bones to eat the marrow inside.

- **The stone tools** used by *Homo habilis* are crude and basic. This hominid was the first toolmaker, but, hardly surprisingly, it was not a skilled one.

- **But making** these early stone tools was still a challenging task—the toolmaker needed to strike one rock with another so that it would produce a single, sharp flake rather than shattering into many pieces.

▼ Homo ergaster *used hammers made of bone to produce thinner and sharper flakes of stone.*

- **Toolmaking requires** considerable intelligence. It involves the use of memory, as well as the ability to plan ahead and to solve abstract problems.

- *Homo ergaster's* tools were much more advanced. This hominid made teardrop shaped, symmetrical hand axes called "Acheulean axes," after the place in France where similar axes have been discovered from a later period.

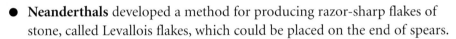

Flint ax

- **Neanderthals** developed a method for producing razor-sharp flakes of stone, called Levallois flakes, which could be placed on the end of spears.

- **This method** required great precision and dexterity. While modern humans have a much broader range of skills, they would be very hard pushed to produce such tools themselves.

- **Modern humans** developed the greatest variety of tools. Cro-Magnon tools include knives, spearpoints, and engraving tools.

- **Cro-Magnon humans** also began to make tools from materials other than stone, including wood, bones, antlers, and ivory.

▲▶ Homo sapiens' *tools became more and more complex. They incorporated different materials, such as twine in the ax (above) and, in this saw (right), flint teeth held in place by resin.*

Hunting

- *Homo erectus* was one of the earliest human hunters. Other hominids that came before it, like *Homo habilis,* may have hunted small or lame animals, but they mostly scavenged other animals' kills.

- *Homo erectus* used fire to drive animals into traps. They also developed handaxes, which they used to kill animals or butcher them once they were dead.

- **But it was the Neanderthals** that excelled in hunting—a skill they developed during the ice ages of the Pleistocene Epoch (1.6–0.01 mya).

- **Hunting** developed into a way of providing not only food, but also clothing (animal skins) and materials for tools (bones, horns, and hooves).

- **Neanderthals** used nets or spears to catch spawning fish. They also hunted seals by spearing them through holes in the ice or by throwing spears at them.

- **In the 1990s,** finds of Neanderthal weapons in Boxgrove, England, showed the full range of this species' hunting arsenal. They include axes, slicing knives, cutting blades, and slashing blades.

- **As well as hunting** for meat, hominids also gathered wild fruits, vegetables, and nuts.

- **Another Neanderthal site,** at Schöningen in Germany, preserved the remains of nine polished wooden spears, made from a spruce tree.

- **Each of these spears** was over 6.5 ft (2 m) long, and was designed to be thrown like a javelin.

- *Homo sapiens* developed new weapons for hunting, including the bow and arrow, the blowpipe, and the boomerang.

▼ *Early humans developed more and more sophisticated methods of killing animals, including weapons, traps, and fire.*

Index

Index

Index

Index

Index

Index

Index

Index